Living Much More Through Buying Much Less

an invitation to deeper values

Fírinn Taisdeal

Living Much More Through Buying Much Less
© 2015 by Fírinn Taisdeal

All rights reserved. No part of this book may be reproduced or transmitted in any form or by any means without prior written permission of the author.

ISBN-13: 978-0-9822868-1-4
ISBN-10: 0982286813

Dedication

To everyone who ever gave me a good idea.

Thank you.

Living Much More Through Buying Much Less

Table of Contents

Foreword   viii

Introduction   x

Two notes of warning   xiii

PART ONE: YOU AND YOUR STUFF   1

Just how much stuff do you have?   1

Why exactly did you buy all that stuff?   2

How did you come to want all that stuff?   2

What is your stuff doing to you?   3

Do you own your stuff, or does your stuff own you?   6

Do you think you're your stuff?   7

Is your stuff making you stupid?   8

Just how much did all that stuff actually cost you?   12

So what if you worked hard for all that stuff?   13

Do you buy stuff out of boredom?   13

Do you buy stuff because you didn't choose to think of anything better to do?   14

Do you buy stuff because you feel inadequate as a person?   15

Do you buy stuff because you're afraid of dying?   17

Do you truly know who you are, apart from your stuff?   19

What is your total cost to the natural world?   19

Do you have demonic possessions?   21

Do you have a storage space for your stuff?   22

You don't actually need all that stuff, do you?   22

You are rarely, if ever, buying just one thing 23

The effect of your possessions on other people 25

The effect on you and other people of what you buy for them 27

"Retail therapy" is about as therapeutic as heroin 28

Blindly accepting the injection of alien desires is not a dignified way to live 29

Conclusion of Part One 30

TRANSITION: A NEW RELATIONSHIP WITH STUFF 32

Advantages of having less stuff 32

For every item, keep in mind the advantages of not owning it 34

Owning it doesn't mean you have to keep it 37

If you haven't used it in a year, get rid of it 37

Excellent ways to get rid of stuff 38

Make your riddance truly good 40

Advantages of buying less stuff 41

Choose any new stuff thoughtfully and carefully 41

Every desire is actually a desire for a feeling 45

PART TWO: DEEPER VALUES 47

Transition toward deeper values 48

Develop and deepen your relationship with truth 51

Don't believe your own fibs 53

Make the deep effort to truly understand yourself 55

Challenge yourself 56

Choose useful experiences 59

Expand your mind 63

Develop your curiosity 64

Develop your imagination   65

Work to become more creative   67

Develop and refine your judgment   68

Carefully choose noble commitments   69

Learn to love the small, modest, free and unencumbered   70

Expand your identity   74

Expand your identity specifically through travel   80

Imagine yourself as a different person   82

Develop a deep relationship with art   84

Acquire useful skills   85

Invest in new capabilities   86

Build financial strength and flexibility   87

Cultivate the virtue of frugality   88

Cultivate the virtue of modesty   89

Develop your relationships   90

Give gifts of love, attention and understanding   92

Productive activities requiring little or no resources   93

Always think of something better to do   94

Seek out and ask yourself excellent, important questions   95

Learn to appreciate everything more deeply   96

Have fun thinking   98

Study a worthy subject in depth   99

Replace bad habits with much better habits   101

Seek out relationships specifically with people who give you new ideas and help you become a better, more capable person 102

Deliberately seek out exchange of valuable information   103

Thank anyone who deserves thanks   104

Give what you don't need to others individually, in the moment   104
Don't watch television–at all   106
Conduct focused, valid and worthwhile research on the web   107
Read books from the library   108
Decide on something truly productive to imagine 109
Let your mind to drift, and watch what it does, and tends to do   111
Deepen your relationship with the natural world 113
Work to fully understand your body   114
Improve your health   116
Change your state by means of your body   118
Invent productive, fun activities with other people, minus stuff   119
Become a certified stuffologist   120
Thank you   121
Web site for Living Much More   121

Appendix: A few favorite possessions   122

Foreword

This book emerged from a fundamental observation; past a certain point, possessions have very little to do with happiness. Possessions also have nothing at all to do with whether one is a good person, an educated person, a cultured person, or a productive member of society.

Yet our entire society emphasizes acquisition of material possessions above all else. We are exhorted ever more frequently by ubiquitous advertising to buy products which more often than not have an inverse relation to positive values of any kind. Many of the products we are encouraged to buy are harmful–to ourselves, to society, to the natural world–yet we are urged to conform through mindless purchasing of yet more of these products.

In our mania to acquire, we have taken little note of what we have lost: deeper values, self-respect, confidence in our society, confidence in each other, confidence in our future together. These are major losses, yet the mania continues, and without reflection, without restraint.

This small book is an invitation to a much richer world than that of shallow material acquisition: a world of the deeper values of the mind and of culture; of appreciation for phenomena great and small; of deep curiosity and the respect that grows from deep curiosity; of development of oneself as a person; of living in relation to ethical and moral ideals. It is also an invitation of another kind: an invitation to freedom.

We tend to think of freedom as the absence of restrictions imposed on us by others. Yet what if the restrictions are unrecognized restrictions of the mind and spirit? What if we have unknowingly imposed restrictions on our own awareness, and remain unaware of those restrictions? Can we be considered truly free when our awareness is confined to a narrow band of conformity, when we are entirely unaware of valid choices apart from the destructive, thoughtless norm?

That is no freedom. Unwitting conformity is no freedom.

If you have not questioned the values and norms of your society, right down to the most fundamental hidden assumptions, you are a prisoner, a slave, a robot, and you don't even know it.

Yet what is this thing we call "society?" Where did it come from? Did it just appear at random all of a sudden? Who is responsible for it?

Thus, a second fundamental insight formed the basis of this book:

Society is not something you are subject to. Society is something you create, with every choice you make. Better choices mean a better society.

I urge you to make better choices. We all can. We all should.

See you on the other side.

Introduction
If you bought this book, I'm truly sorry. In a way, this book is just one more thing you bought, adding to all the other stuff you've bought throughout your life. Yet I hope that this little book is unique among your possessions, for the following reason; this one purchase could transform your life, by transforming your relationship with all your other possessions, and helping you to become a stronger and more capable person, completely independent of anything you own. If that is the case for you after reading this book, please pass the book along to someone, and ask them to pass it along to someone else. If, on a larger level, this book helps to any degree to reduce the truly amazing amount of junk people buy, then the book itself was worth its own production.

Throughout the book, I'll refer to all your possessions, of no matter what type, simply as your "stuff." A person's "stuff" comes in many forms, with many different characteristics and effects. Some people have a truly astonishing amount and range of stuff, and most of us have a whole heap of stuff, more than we can even keep track of easily. Yet absolutely all of your stuff shares one fundamental characteristic:

Your stuff is not you.

That's right, your stuff is not you, and you are not your stuff. You have a certain relationship with your stuff, and that relationship can change, and can be changed, for better or for worse. This books is all about you, your stuff, your relationship with your stuff, and most of all how to change your relationship with your stuff so that you expand the possibilities in your life.

Why do people buy so much stuff? People buy stuff in part because doing so brings a sense of new and expanded possibilities, even if only for a short time, even when in many cases possessions actually tie use down, limit us, confine us. Yet you can achieve a far greater, more lasting and more genuine experience of new and expanded possibilities by freeing yourself from your stuff, and ultimately from possessions in general. This freedom and expansion of possibilities is of far greater extent and far greater durability and utility than any purchase you could ever make.

To be absolutely clear, I am not advocating that you not own anything. I am not advocating a lack of possessions. What I am advocating is a thoughtful, satisfying and productive relationship with possessions. I am advocating a much deeper experience of life through changing your relationship with your possessions, and advocating valid pride in the conscious evaluation of your relationship with everything you own, and the values represented by what you own.

Yes, your possessions do represent your values. Do you know what your values are? Have you ever defined your values clearly? Could you sit down and right them out? If you have never defined your values clearly, this book may help you to do so, in part through a detailed process of evaluating your possessions, and your relationship with your possessions.

On a larger level, I am also advocating the development of a society based on much deeper values than the shallow, mindless, materialist conformity currently dominant. At this point in history, our society has produced tremendous material wealth, though unevenly distributed in the extreme. Because distribution of material wealth has become more and more skewed toward the already wealthy, the proportion of people whose material circumstances have worsened has actually increased; despite an overall increase in wealth, more people are worse off. Thus we are now living a painful contradiction; our worship of wealth and material success has actually produced a decrease in wealth for most people. Thus even on its own basis of evaluation, that of material success, our society is a failure.

The much deeper failure is that our society has not produced a set of values worthy of respect. Our society has also not yet produced a way of life that is not destructive to the natural systems on which we ultimately depend. In fundamental ways, our society remains weak, poorly developed, of shoddy character, with a tenuous relationship to truth and honesty, and lacking almost entirely the honest and accurate self-evaluation that is necessary for improvement.

Which is better, a society with tremendous and growing capability on all levels, as well as everything it needs materially, or a society with a vast amount of of personal possessions but little capability on other levels? The answer to that question is obvious, and the question itself is obvious, yet you may never have seen such a question before. That such a question of such fundamental importance would be a rarity is a symptom of just how sick with consumerism our society has become.

The ultimate goal of this book is to present a vision of a very different society, a society with far more capability on every level: mentally, emotionally, spiritually, and in knowledge, skill and expertise, but most of all in far better judgment in the most important matters, based on values far deeper and more comprehensive than the crude question of whether all of us can ever more easily buy even more junk.

Society is the result of individual choices, aggregated. If you want to improve society, it makes no sense at all to not first start with yourself. The change, the improvement must start with you. Where else would it start? Do you think society is going to suddenly improve without your having to do anything? Some people don't like that idea.

Thus, this book is not for everyone, for more than one reason. The many, many people who are incurably shallow materialists will, by their very nature, be unable to respond to or even to understand the content of this book. The many people who would prefer to complain about society while asking nothing of themselves are also not compatible with the content of this book. Only those who understand vividly the power of personal transformation and personal example will be able to recognize the value of what is offered here.

The book is divided into two major parts. Part one is an assessment of your relationship with your stuff. Depending on the details of your emotional and psychological relationship with your stuff, you may find this part challenging at times. We all exist on a set of spectra, from compulsive "ridders" to compulsive hoarders, from minimalists to maximalists, from modest to exhibitionist, from grossly thoughtless to deeply thoughtful. We all respond differently to different conditions, and respond differently at different points in our life. Yet we can always make conscious choices as to how we relate to our possessions.

In evaluating and changing your relationship with your possessions, it's helpful to keep certain fundamental questions in mind:

- What expands your capabilities as a person?
- What limits you as a person?
- What inspires you?
- What ties you down?
- What clogs your mind, and clouds your soul?
- What clears your mind, and frees your soul?
- What increases and what decreases the possibilities in your life?
- When you buy something, what are you also giving up?
- What values do your possessions represent?

Part two of the book presents a world of positive options, completely apart from material possessions, with emphasis on developing new capabilities as a person, and building an identity based on values, not things.

Freedom awaits you.

Two notes of warning
I have a responsibility to warn you about two aspects of this book.

Warning #1
The message of the book is strong. The message of the book is also serious. The tone of the book corresponds to the strength and seriousness of the message. If you are someone who insists on being spoken to as though everything you do is absolutely wonderful, and nothing about you could possibly be improved, this book is definitely not for you, so please read no further. However, if you are someone who welcomes interesting challenges, including challenges about yourself, your behavior, and your values, I think you're in for a great experience.

Like most people, I have been through particular struggles in relation to material belongings: everything from faddish conformity I later regretted, to carefully saving for something I should never have wanted in the first place, to lust for accumulation, to the need to purge, to fetishistic adoration of beautiful objects, and lots else in between.

Several years ago I finally took a critical look at my relationship with material possessions, and made a disciplined, consistent effort to study and understand what was driving my own behavior. This was not an easy process, nor necessarily pleasant or flattering, but it was tremendously illuminating, tremendously worthwhile, and ultimately liberating to an extent I still find amazing every day.

I now own much less than I did before, but I live a much better life, and deeply enjoy and appreciate the possessions I have chosen to keep. I also have no conflict at all in relation to my much smaller burden of possessions, and have a valid pride in the ethical basis of my relation to possessions in general. To be blunt, I worked very hard to become less of an idiot.

I did all the work of evaluating my own relationship to possessions, so now I am able to form clear, strong judgments about how other people relate to their possessions. You may feel uncomfortable with these judgments. If that's the case, I invite you to take that as a sign that the deeper truth is that you are not completely proud of your own relationship with your possessions. That's for you to settle within yourself in your own way, in your own time. I wish you the best of success in doing so.

Warning #2
If you read this book with an open heart, it will change you, and may radically transform your relationship with your possessions, and with possessions in general. Not all of this process of change will be easy, or flattering, but that's exactly how the process operates; you encounter observations and insights that cause you to question your choices, which leads to discomfort, which leads to motivation toward change. If you persist in this process, through many iterations, you eventually become very good at it and the process goes much faster, and becomes fascinating, deeply satisfying, and a source of pride.

You may eventually come to view this process as necessary, on a moral level, because we are all far less than perfect, and therefore all have a lot of work to do on ourselves. To deny this would be dishonest and irresponsible. So please embrace the process, lean into it, learn to enjoy and appreciate it, welcome the insights it brings, and go on to greater things and a better life as a result.

During this process, you may experience serious and perhaps sudden shifts in your attitude toward your possessions. It's even possible, for instance, that you will begin to feel hostility toward certain possessions which have too strong a hold over you, or which represent values that, when you consider them consciously, are not values you can respect. That's completely normal, and a fundamental aspect of the transition away from a thoughtless relationship with possessions. After all, the word "possession" has two distinct meanings, but the meanings are clearly related. Please keep in mind, throughout the book, this dual meaning of "possession."

Exorcism is not an easy matter. Stick with it. Free yourself.

PART ONE: YOU AND YOUR STUFF

"Going to a junkyard is a sobering experience. There you can see the ultimate destination of almost everything we desire."

— Roger von Oech (1948-)

Just how much stuff do you have?
Try to think of everything you own. No, I mean *everything* you own: absolutely every object you consider your possession, from the largest to the smallest, from things that have been with you since childhood to the latest object you added to your household. Would you be able to list absolutely everything you own, without going through all your stuff? Probably not. If you can't even remember everything you own, then much of what you own clearly doesn't matter, and is just clogging up your life.

To gain perspective on everything you own, consider the following:

- Accurate to a pound, how much do your possessions weigh, in total?
- How much cubic space would be required to contain all of them?
- What is their total number, counting even the smallest items?
- How many of them could you lift and carry a mile by yourself?
- How much money did you waste in acquiring them?
- What else could you have done, if you hadn't wasted all that money?
- What could you do if you had all that money now?
- Could you dispose of them without any harm to the natural world?
- How do you feel now, just thinking all this over?

You may have just experienced a bit of shock. That's good. That's an excellent beginning. Let's go further.

Why exactly did you buy all that stuff?
How did you come to buy all the things you have? Did you truly think over each purchase? How many times have you bought something and then regretted it? How many things have you bought, used once or twice, and never used again? Perhaps you rid yourself of belongings periodically and so have not accumulated a lot of possessions, but if you're like most people, you own quite a few things you can't even remember buying, let alone when, let alone why.

Can you fully justify everything you own? If not, I suggest it's time to examine exactly how you came to own all those things. This involves tracing the origins of your desires, a process which can generate illuminating, if often unflattering insights. Again, stick with it.

How did you come to want all that stuff?
This question is actually less straightforward and potentially more embarrassing than it first appears. For each object you acquired because you wanted it, can you trace the exact origin of your desire for that object? If you are honest with yourself, you will have to admit that in many cases the origin of your desire for many of your possessions is nothing to be proud of, and often indicates conformity, envy, competition, social pressure, or even susceptibility to the insidious psychological ploys of advertising and marketing. It's not easy to admit these things, but if you want greater freedom of choice, honesty with yourself is part of the cost.

So for some of the more questionable of your possessions–and only you know what those are–I invite you to ask yourself the following questions:

- Do you know exactly how and why you came to want that thing?
- How did you first learn of it?
- Was it through an advertisement, or through a friend or acquaintance?
- Did you want it because you truly needed it, or did you allow yourself to be convinced you "needed" something you actually didn't need?
- What was the emotional motivation of the desire? Greed? Envy? Competition? Conformity? Not wanting to be left out? Not

wanting to feel like a loser because you didn't have the thing that all your friends had? Something else?
- When you look at that object now, do you feel pride, self-respect, or something less flattering?

Most of us, as a matter of pride, are reluctant to admit the unflattering reasons we came to desire certain possessions. Yet what true pride can there possibly be in shielding yourself dishonestly from an unflattering truth about yourself? I suggest reversing your attitude about such admissions. Make it a matter of pride to be honest with yourself. Make honesty with yourself your source of pride, particularly when that honesty causes you to question yourself, because that is when it matters most.

This exercise of asking yourself honestly the precise reasons you acquired each of your possessions is one of the most valuable skills you can develop. The process of reviewing honestly the precise reasons you acquired certain possessions leads directly to an examination of values: the good and bad reasons behind desire for possessions, what reasons for ownership are worthy of respect, and what reasons for ownership are not worthy of respect.

If you're willing to take the time, reviewing your major possessions and writing down the exact reasons you acquired the object and whether you respect those reasons or not will quickly transform for the better your evaluation of possible new possessions, and quite probably cause you to want to reduce your burden of possessions. It can also save you a ton of money.

What is your stuff doing to you?

Everything you own affects you, one way or another, to one degree or another. Your possessions can have a wide range of effects on you, positive or negative, subtle or obvious, shallow or very, very deep.

For instance, many people who own a car are very strongly affected by their car, the experience of driving, and the burdens and hassles of car ownership. Anyone who has to regularly commute by car is affected by that experience, often in ways that are not entirely clear to them, on a conscious level. I've known people who became habitually irritable and even depressed because of the amount of time they had to spend driving, yet failed to identify the cause.

Owning a home is also not an exclusively positive experience, in many ways. Home ownership is often referred to as a "dream," but not all dreams are good, and dreams can also be or become nightmares. Some homes become sinkholes of personal finance, but that's only one aspect of home ownership. Another major aspect is the cost of time and attention, which could have been otherwise spent, perhaps more productively spent. Yet another aspect, which becomes obsessive for certain people, is comparison with others. This sort of comparison becomes a disease for some people, a mental and emotional disease, which destroys their happiness and appreciation for what they do have, and not just in material possessions.

Another example is television. While watching television might seem a relatively harmless activity, the effects of television are deep, less than obvious, and bring with them further implications. What is the fundamental purpose of television? The fundamental purpose of television is to convince you that you need things which in nearly all cases you do not need at all, and which will weaken your finances, waste your time, impair your judgment, and ultimately turn you into a zombie more easily conducted toward further mindless purchases. That is the fundamental purpose of television. Those glowing boxes are now inexpensive–except in the cost to your mind, your soul, and in the loss of every hour you could have spent more productively, and to your own benefit.

So I invite you to reflect, to ask yourself some serious questions:

- Have you analyzed the effect of your possessions on you?
- How much time have your possessions consumed, and to exactly what purpose?
- Were those purposes truly positive, truly productive?
- How have your possessions affected your mind?
- Have your possessions your mind to expand, or caused it to contract?
- Have your possessions expanded your awareness, or caused it to contract? (Not exactly the same as the previous question.)
- How have your possessions led you to desire other possessions?
- Have your possessions reduced the possibilities in other areas of your life?
- How have your possessions changed your attitudes?
- How have your possessions affected your judgment?

- How have your possessions affected your relationship with yourself?
- How have your possessions affected your relationship with other people?
- Have your possessions caused you to become more of a conformist?
- Have your possessions caused you to become more courageous, or less courageous? In what ways?
- Have your possessions caused you to feel defensive, because now you're worried about losing them? How does that affect the rest of your life, as well as your relationship with yourself?
- Have your possessions caused you to compare yourself to other people who have bigger, supposedly better possessions? How does that affect the rest of your life, as well as your relationship with yourself?
- Have your possessions increased your self-respect, or in some ways reduced it? How does that affect the rest of your life, as well as your relationship with yourself?
- Have your possessions deepened your development as a human being, or in some ways reduced your development as a human being? How does that affect the rest of your life, as well as your relationship with yourself?

Exercise: Take stock of the effects, on you, of your possessions
The instructions for this exercise are simple. The exercise itself is difficult. For each of the questions listed immediately above, write out a complete, thoughtful and honest answer. Take your time, and insist on complete honesty with yourself.

Do you own your stuff, or does your stuff own you?
Some people are owned by their possessions, in ways that vary from comical to troubling to truly pathetic. I've known a few "homeowners" who are actually owned by their homes; they are slaves to maintenance, worry, compulsive social comparison, expansion and remodeling, often leading to the further loss of freedom and sometimes heavy debt. I've known people who were owned by their cars, with every year bringing a new car loan and further debt, and every weekend spent cleaning and waxing and fiddling and primping. A huge number of people are owned by their television, and this ownership by their television involves not just huge amounts of wasted time, but also a loss of mental acuity, loss of perspective, and loss of self-respect. The television also convinced them, in their stupor, to buy additional products of many kinds, with further implications for use of time, loss of mental acuity, loss of perspective, and loss of self-respect.

PART ONE: YOU AND YOUR STUFF

Exercise: Can you imagine?
Try to imagine doing without certain things you own, that you don't actually use. An obvious example would be exercise equipment. Most exercise equipment is purchased, used a few times if at all, then left unused for years while inflicting a subtle or not so subtle burden of guilt on the purchaser, after finally being given up, often when it has deteriorated so much as to be useless to anyone else as well. Perhaps you've never purchased exercise equipment, but chances are there are other things that you've bought but no longer use, and are still holding on to, even though you recognize that it does not make sense to do so.

In many cases, as soon as you consider the idea of giving the item up, you may notice a powerful urge to try to justify keeping it, even though you don't use it; you may invent all kinds of stories about how you really need it, how you're really going to use it eventually, if only this, and if only that. You may even find yourself pledging to set aside time you can't actually afford, and won't actually set aside, just in order to keep the item.

But move on with the process, imagining that you no longer have those items. Observe your emotional and psychological and social responses when you imagine yourself without those things. You may observe yourself tempted toward less than full honesty as to whether you actually will use them any time soon. That's normal and natural, and just information for you about your own responses. The point is to learn from the process, on as many levels as possible, to gain the advantages of becoming more realistic about what your current possessions, and how you go about choosing new possessions.

Do you think you're your stuff?
You are not your stuff. However, if you're like most people, you probably have some confusion about this. Some people identify deeply with their possession, other people less so. Many people who are deeply attached to their stuff no longer have the slightest idea of who they are, apart from their stuff. If you asked them to imagine themselves with none of their stuff, you might trigger a panic attack in them, because they wouldn't know what would be left of them.

The question of fundamental importance in any case however, is this: Do you know precisely who you are, entirely apart from all your stuff? Are you sure? If suddenly every last possession of yours vanished forever, would you still know exactly who you are?

Is your stuff making you stupid?
I don't mean to be rude, but there is a strong probability that, to one extent or another, at least some of your stuff has made you at least a little bit stupid. Some of your stuff has probably made you somewhat stupid, and some of your stuff has perhaps made you very stupid, in certain ways. You are not alone. It happens to all of us, to some degree. Behold the catalog of types of stupidity, where possessions are concerned.

Stupid use of time
Certain stuff takes a lot of our time. In many cases it doesn't make any sense to spend all that time on that stuff, and yet we do it because we're used to it, because we try to justify having that stuff by using that stuff, because it's hard to imagine how we would spend our time if we didn't spend it on that stuff, and because we fear the disorientation and anxiety that can well up from gaps in our use of time.

Have you ever known someone who spends much of their free time "maintaining" something that they don't need, and that actually interferes with their having much of a life otherwise? Have you ever known someone with a hobby that consumes a lot of their time, but provides no benefit other than as a hedge against confusion over what else to do? Is there anything you spend a lot of time on, but know is not a good use your time?

Possessions in and of themselves can strongly influence and even directly determine how you spend your time. To put it bluntly, if someone didn't have a TV, would they ever sit down to watch it? Yet someone with a TV, simply because the TV is there, and the couch is there, and the remote is there, and the 200+ channels of "programming" (consider the double meaning of that term) are there, may end up spending many hours a week parked in front of the ZIU (Zombie Indoctrination Unit), absorbing new messages about what else to desire, and therefore what else to buy, and use, and spend time on, and bug their friends to buy, too.

Stupid use of attention
Every moment of our attention is valuable. Decisions, conscious or not, about where to direct our attention are the fundamental building blocks of our life. What we pay attention to determines to a large extent the structure of our minds, our attitudes, our understanding of the world, and even what we are able to be aware of, as habits of attention take hold and exclude other possibilities for awareness.

PART ONE: YOU AND YOUR STUFF

Our attention is strictly limited. Each choice we make to pay attention to something means we are choosing not to pay attention to many other things, which means that each choice to pay attention to something actually means many, many lost opportunities. Therefore what we pay attention to had better be much more important than what we are choosing not to pay attention to, or we're being horribly stupid.

Certain possessions invite truly stupid use of attention. I can't tell you what those possessions are in your case, but if you're honest with yourself, certain of your possessions will stand out as truly bad uses of your attention, especially when you consider what you're giving up by not paying attention to matters of greater importance.

Induction of social stupidity

Some possessions tend to induce social stupidity, whether in the form of insensitivity, reduced awareness, rigid reactions, or the blind assumption that others will be or should be interested in that type of possession. Any possession can have this effect, because the effect is based on the psychology of the person, not on the nature of the object itself, yet some possessions are more likely than others to induce social stupidity.

You may disagree with me, but in my opinion video games are a blatant example of a possession that tends to induce severe social stupidity. In my experience, video games induce all four negative qualities listed at the beginning of this section; the compulsive user of video games is often insensitive to their social environment, has reduced awareness in general, is rigidly insistent on playing the game even in truly inappropriate circumstances, and thinks you're an idiot for not liking it.

Other examples in and around the home abound. Stuff you want can make you truly stupid without even having it yet. Many an otherwise intelligent person became so fixated on their kitchen remodel that severe social stupidity was deeply induced, and over a painfully long period of time: from early consideration of the remodel, with much discussion required, to examining options for the remodel, to negotiations over the remodel with contractors, to interminable forced discussion of color and materials options with friends and acquaintances, to scheduling problems with the contractors, to numerous efforts to solicit awe and admiration for the completed remodel, to regret over certain choices in the remodel, to consideration of yet another remodel.

Stupidity through loss of other valuable abilities
For some possessions, the loss entailed by the possession is indirect, and therefore difficult to discern. Certain possessions, particularly those which consume large amounts of time over an extended period, can cause atrophy of other valuable abilities, purely through exclusion by time constraints. The abilities which atrophy may be unrelated to the possession that has caused the atrophy, so the causal connection between them is not obvious.

Loss of social skills is, however an obvious example of abilities that may be lost due to excessive involvement with certain possessions, but any ability is subject to decay if neglected over a long period of time. Many of us have lost physical abilities because so much of what we own causes us to be seated much more than is healthy: computers, televisions, cars. More subtle losses of ability occur in the realm of the mind and the spirit due to a certain kind of relationship with possessions. For instance, a powerful, active imagination is tremendously valuable, but some possessions tend to destroy or limit our imagination, not develop it. Some possessions tend to contract the mind, not expand it. The ability to be open to new, valuable experience is deeply important, yet there are possessions which have the effect of stunting this ability.

Do you own anything that is causing you to lose valuable abilities?

Stupidity through excessive sentimentality
Sentiment is an essential aspect of human life. Of course we all have things to which we are sentimentally attached. Sometimes the sentiment is of harmless strength, but for some people the bonds of sentiment become bondage to sentiment. I know certain people, for instance who save every tiny memento, every doodad that reminds them of an event, every bauble ever given to them by a long deceased aunt, uncle, grandparent, sibling, co-worker, friend, acquaintance, significant other and even insignificant other. For each object, memories are stored and carefully maintained as to when, where, from whom, and under exactly what circumstances the object was obtained, and the exact words, if any, delivered at the time. The heap of memories becomes an unmovable mountain of extremely detailed, intractable sentiment. They are trapped under that mountain, and yet they keep adding to its mass.

In other cases it is not the number of items to which a restrictive web of sentiment is attached, but a few items, to which powerfully restrictive sentiment is attached. Sometimes the restrictive sentiment is so strong that it warps the person's entire life, and deprives them of precious new possibilities in their life.

Clearly, this is not just normal sentiment in operation, but a disease, a disease that prevents the person from developing further. It's also a form of stupidity. The people I know who contracted that disease and carried it into middle age are completely unable to advance in life; they are embedded in set concrete of sentiment. It's a sad thing to witness.

Stupidity through rigid attachment
I once visited a family whose living room appeared quite normal. Entering the room, I took the first available seat. Suddenly, tension gripped everyone else in the room. A strained silence took hold. After a few moments the daughter in the family stepped gingerly toward me and whispered in my ear "That's my father's chair. No one else is allowed to sit in it. Please sit somewhere else."

In another case, a man I knew gradually became unable to throw away his daily newspaper, which he didn't read because he was too busy "maintaining" his ungainly house. Eventually, after fifty years of this, entire rooms of his house were stacked to the ceiling with newspapers, and much of the house had become unusable. Thus his rigid attachment to his house led to his not reading his newspapers, and his attachment to his newspapers destroyed his beloved house.

Clearly both of these examples are extreme, but it's easy to think of others in our own lives in which a rigid attachment interferes with our judgment and causes damage in our lives, including loss of other opportunities.

Exercise: Does it own you?
This exercise may not apply to you, but please try it anyway. Is there any possession in your life to which you are rigidly attached? If your immediate answer is no, ask yourself whether anyone in your life who knows you well would answer differently about you. Sometimes other people can see things about us that we can't easily see about ourselves, so this exercise of imagining what someone else might say about you can expand your awareness.

If you can identify something in your life to which you are rigidly attached, then realize and accept that you don't own it at all, however much you cling. Instead, it owns you, controls you, and always will until you free yourself from it. Can you imagine freeing yourself from this possession? Can you imagine what you would gain from doing so?

Just how much did all that stuff actually cost you?
Everything you buy means money you gave up or made less accessible. Yet money may be the least of the matter. Everything you buy also involves, by implication, everything you didn't buy that would have been a better, more productive choice. Every time you buy something, you are not only surrendering money, but surrendering all the choices that would have been better than that choice. "Getting" also involves losing, though we generally blind ourselves to what we are losing in the process, because we don't like to think about it.

One of the most severe examples of this is the purchase of a "vacation home." I knew someone who bought a cabin in a mountain town many years ago. He bought the second home because he couldn't resist the egotistical pull of being able to refer to this second home, and the rush of shallow self-esteem this would produce. He felt like a big man, being able to refer to his "vacation home."

After twenty years, the result was that he had never taken a vacation anywhere other than that one terribly uninteresting mountain town, and knew nothing about the rest of the world. Eventually he lost any curiosity about the rest of the world, and became afraid to travel. He then became chronically depressed, but couldn't figure out why. He also ended up nearly a million dollars in debt, in part because he wasn't willing to give up that second home.

The cost of that petty ego trip was extraordinarily high. He thought he was gaining a house he could brag about. Instead he lost every interesting vacation over the course of twenty years that could have fed his mind and his soul, he lost his curiosity, he lost his courage, he lost his financial security, and he lost his ability to think his way out of the terrible situation he had created. He also deprived his entire family of vacations other than to the same boring mountain town for twenty years, and subjected his family to painful outbursts once things started to go off the rails financially.

This is a chilling tale, I know. But the lesson is that all your stuff costs you something, far past its initial purchase price, and some of your stuff can have a truly frightening price tag that is only revealed over time. Beware those possessions that have too strong a hold over you. Beware those possessions you acquired for less than noble reasons. They do not have your best interest in mind. They are not your friends.

So I ask you to seriously consider what you gave up, both materially and in terms of experience, for what you own.

PART ONE: YOU AND YOUR STUFF

Exercise: What did you give up in the process?
For a few of your major possessions, ask yourself seriously and honestly what you gave up or may have given up for that possession. What did that possession cost you, first of all in terms of what else you could have bought that would have been more worthwhile, but also in terms of what that possession cost you in lost opportunities? Could you have concentrated on having important, productive experiences instead of buying that thing? Could you have simply not bought that thing, and chosen to learn some important skills instead? Use your imagination, and use your ability to analyze. If you find yourself filling with regret in some cases, that's actually a good thing, because regret can be truly instructive, if you accept its lessons.

The major point here is to train yourself to understand more deeply the implications of your choices as to possessions, and free yourself from the illusion promoted by society that purchases are always good.

A practical method for doing this on an ongoing basis is to build a spreadsheet which includes entries for all your significant purchases, with columns for briefly defining what you are giving up for that possession. If you are considering any further significant purchases, add them to the spreadsheet for evaluation before making a decision.

So what if you worked hard for all that stuff?
I know plenty of people who work hard. Some of those people who work hard also have a lot of stuff. When I ask them why they work hard, they say it's to have all that stuff. When I ask why they want all this stuff, whether they have time to use it all, whether they might not be better off with a bit less stuff, the answers often are embarrassingly weak. Finally it becomes clear that they want all that stuff in part to justify how hard they work for it. Thus, the endless loop: they work hard for the stuff because they want it, but they want it because they worked hard for it. When and where does it end? Are you in the same kind of loop?

Do you buy stuff out of boredom?
Buying stuff out of boredom is so common that we have come to accept it without reflection. We accept both the practice of buying out of boredom and the word "boredom" without reflection. What exactly is "boredom," though? Most of us experience boredom as an irritating or even painful lack of interesting external stimuli. We think of

boredom as the result of an uninteresting environment. Rarely do we perceive boredom as our own lack of creativity, but that's actually what it is.

If you choose to experience boredom instead as a reminder of your responsibility to think creatively, as your responsibility to create an interesting environment for yourself, you experience a challenge, a challenge to become and remain more creative. This in itself is a much more interesting experience than that of complaining that you're "bored." The experience may be just as frustrating, but the frustration is with yourself, and the eventual result if you make the transition to this new attitude toward managing boredom is greater confidence in yourself, greater imagination, and greater embrace of responsibility in general.

So the next time you feel bored, particularly if you respond to the boredom by suddenly wanting to head out the mall, or "browse" on Amazon, just pull back from the abyss, and cultivate your creativity instead. If you make this a habit, you'll actually have much more to show for it in the end.

Do you buy stuff because you didn't choose to think of anything better to do?

This is similar to buying stuff out of boredom, but not quite the same. You may not be bored, you may not be in the thick of the frustration of boredom, yet still you go out and buy something. That means, by definition, that you didn't think of anything better to do. Not thinking of anything better to do doesn't necessarily mean you can't think of anything better to do. Developing the habit of choosing to think of something better to do than just buying something offers major advantages financially, and in terms of both opportunity and personal capability.

Exercise: What would have been a better choice?

Think of something you bought, perhaps something you now regret buying. What choice could you have made that would have not only not involved buying anything, but would have been a better, more interesting, more productive choice?

PART ONE: YOU AND YOUR STUFF

Do you buy stuff because you feel inadequate as a person?
Yes, I know that question sounds harsh, but it's one of the most serious questions in the entire book. Many people feel inadequate in many ways. Sometimes those feelings are not valid, but sometimes they are. If you feel inadequate about something, but shouldn't, the goal is to perceive yourself more accurately. If you feel inadequate because you actually are inadequate in some way, that's an entirely different matter. Clearly, in that case, the goal should be to work on yourself.

That's not what most people do, however. Instead, they try to compensate, to mask the feelings, to fool themselves, to distract themselves. Those responses just create additional complexity, new problems, and a bigger mess. I've known quite a few people whose response to feelings of inadequacy was to buy stuff. Buying stuff and owning stuff makes them feel important, as a way of masking deeper, unflattering feelings about themselves. This almost always backfires eventually, though it may take a long time for that to happen. In some cases the extent of the eventual mess, and the damage to their own lives and relationships, is absolutely amazing.

I look back on a few things I bought a long time ago, and I just cringe. It was as though I was trying to prove to myself that I was special, that I was important, because what I was feeling about myself at the time was exactly the opposite. Instead of facing my feelings and fears, and working on myself, I just went out and bought something that provided a temporary and ultimately empty boost to my ego. The result was that I not only wasted money, and wasted time not facing the actual issue, but felt even worse about myself later for having been a coward.

After a few rounds of witnessing my own weakness, evasion and stupidity, and the negative results of my behavior, I worked hard to face the underlying issues. Eventually I built consistent habits of self-questioning that helped me never to make purchases based on a misguided need to feel better about myself.

So don't buy the stuff. Deal with yourself first. You'll eventually feel much better, though definitely not at first. The big payoff comes much later, if you really do the work; you'll have valid self-esteem, and you'll make much better decisions about what to buy, and what not buy, and can take pride in that.

Exercise: Can you face yourself?
This is a very tough exercise, but one of the most rewarding, ultimately. There are many ways to go about it. One of the most direct ways is to make a list of everything you don't like about yourself, all the ways you feel inadequate. Naturally, it's best to keep this list completely private. This is for you, and for you alone.

Write in invisible ink if you must, but just go ahead and describe in complete detail every way you feel you fall short. Try to be purely accurate. Don't get involved in putting yourself down, and don't use pejorative terms. Just describe accurately the ways you wish you were better. Next, for each negative aspect you listed, describe a few actions you could take that would help you begin to improve that aspect. Finally, give yourself some hearty pats on the back for being one of the few people in the history of all of humanity who has ever actually done this.

You will probably find that having done this exercise even once, your outlook and behavior will change for the better. It's a good idea to return to this exercise again and again. Each time you'll be able to observe what progress you've made, and where you need to concentrate your effort. If you do this exercise repeatedly, you will also notice your attitude toward possessions changing; when you respect yourself more, when you have no need to prove anything to anyone, possessions and acquisition have less of a hold on you, and you are better able to make your own conscious choices, for your own conscious reasons.

Do you buy stuff because you're afraid of dying?
Shocking question, I know, but this question only applies to certain types of purchases, and only to certain people. If you can say with complete confidence that this question does not apply to you in any way, never has, and never will, please jump ahead. However, if you think there is even the slightest chance that this question might apply to you, or might apply to you at some point, please continue.

Sorry for the bad news, but every one of us is going to die. Some of us accept this completely, and have no illusions about it in general, yet nearly all of us lie to ourselves in various ways about how much time we have, and what we will be able to accomplish in the time we have left. We also are willfully unclear with ourselves about probabilities: the probability of accidents, the probability of problems with our health, the probability of other random events that may cut our lives short.

I have known a few people who, it is quite apparent, try to defend themselves emotionally from awareness of mortality through acquisition. In some cases this takes the form of a compulsion to buy the latest shiny product. In others it's compulsive "improvements" to their already overly improved house. In still others it takes the form, for instance, of an oddly strong interest in antiques. In each case the underlying motivation is an effort to distract themselves from their own mortality. The shiny new product helps them feel shiny new themselves, at least for a time. The "improvement" of their house helps them feel, briefly, that the house of their own body is not gradually deteriorating. The antiques offer an implied fantasy that somehow they themselves will be preserved.

This behavior in general is subtle, though I have also seen some grotesque examples. In every case however, it's an evasion. We are all going to die. It makes no sense to waste what little time you have to be alive pretending you're not going to die, or pretending the unpredictability of life is any less than it is. Full awareness of mortality should be invigorating. It's *your* life. It's *your* time here. Be bold with your life. Be bold with your time here. Take pride in the honest recognition of risk and uncertainty during your ride.

As an addendum, keep in mind that after you're gone, other people are going to be dealing with all your possessions, one way or another. You'll be dead when they're looking at your stuff, but at least you can avoid some embarrassing conclusions about why you bought all that stuff.

Exercise: Imagine your stuff after you're dead
Imagine you're dead. You died a couple of weeks ago, there was a lovely memorial service and certain people miss you deeply, but now it's time for certain people to deal with all your belongings. Imagine that you are now able to watch everything those people do in dealing with your stuff. You can even watch their thoughts, reactions and feelings.

As they go through your stuff, what will they find? What will they think of you as they go through every last bit of your stuff? Will their respect for you increase, or decrease? Will your respect for yourself increase, or decrease?

PART ONE: YOU AND YOUR STUFF

Do you truly know who you are, apart from your stuff?
Many people identify so strongly with what they own, even though true ownership of anything at all is an illusion, that it's difficult to discern the boundary between their possessions and their "self." Everyone operates on a spectrum between the poles of full identification with possessions, and no identification with possessions. Where are you on that spectrum? Where do you think you should be on that spectrum? What advantages or disadvantages do you see in various levels of identification with possessions?

Exercise: What is left of you?
Imagine yourself sitting in a large field, knowing that you own absolutely nothing. Everything you ever had is gone, washed away forever, and cannot be replaced. You don't even have any clothes. Do you still know who you are? What would you know about yourself? What would suddenly be unclear to you? Who exactly would you be, without any possessions?

What is your total cost to the natural world?
Can you think of any object you own that improved the natural environment during its production? Probably not. Nearly everything you own has its basis in damage to the natural world. We all still need to own things, but it would be dishonest not to acknowledge that nearly all of our possessions result in damage to the natural world on which we ultimately depend. As a matter of honesty, dignity and morality, it's crucial to take responsibility for the fundamental fact that the extent of your possessions also represents the extent of the cost to the natural world of your choices in life.

You exist at a cost to other creatures. There is an inescapable moral dimension to this. Are you so worthy as a being, so noble and so elevated and so productive and so generous, that other creatures must give up their lives for you? Do you really believe that? Do you believe yourself so much more worthy in every way that any other creature must sacrifice its life for you? If you do, is there any limit to how many other creatures have to die for you? How would you define that limit?

Your possessions also exist at a cost to other creatures. Do other creatures also have to die in order for you to have as many possessions as possible? Exactly how many different creatures, and of what kinds, have to surrender their lives for your possessions?

Exercise: Estimate your total cost to the natural world

In this exercise, I ask that you think deeply about exactly where everything you own came from, and what was involved in making it. What resources were extracted to produce your possessions? What damage was done to natural systems in the process of that extraction? How much energy was required for extraction of those natural resources, transport for manufacturing, the manufacturing itself, transport to point of purchase, and transport to your home? How much damage was done to natural systems to produce all that energy? How much pollution was produced, all along the entire chain of events leading to that item being in your home?

To put the matter bluntly, how many other creatures may have had their lives or their homes damaged, destroyed or polluted for the sake of your possessions? Use your imagination. Use it vividly. Imagine the homes of various animals, plants, and other organisms degraded, poisoned, destroyed, just so that you could own that sorry little... whatever it is.

This may quite quickly feel overwhelming. If that's the case, narrow your scope. Choose just one major possession, or just the possessions in one room. The point is to begin to take responsibility for your effect on the natural world, and the natural systems on which we ultimately depend.

If you can think of any possession of yours, anything at all, which actually benefits the natural world and other creatures, please start by giving yourself credit for that. I tend a small garden, and try to make it a home for as many creatures as possible. This is paltry compensation for the fact that nearly everything else I own came at the expense of the natural world. One of my personal goals is to shift the proportion of my possessions toward those which benefit and enhance the natural world, instead of degrading it. I hope you'll make that a goal for yourself as well.

PART ONE: YOU AND YOUR STUFF

Do you have demonic possessions?
Play on words aside, I've found it helpful to think of certain possessions not as objects I own, but as objects that happen to be in my life that want something from me. It is an interesting mental and emotional exercise, where certain possessions are concerned, to ask yourself "What the hell does this thing want from me?" Some possessions seem to have a demonic power. Sometimes it's their power to completely take over our attention, perhaps for long periods of time. Sometimes it's their power to warp our emotions, or our relationships, or our view of ourselves. Some possessions have a peculiar power to make us talk about them, idiotically and interminably, to just about anyone. Some possessions sap our will, while hypnotizing us into buying more of them. Some possessions tempt us toward an evil way of looking down on people who don't have those possessions.

So I ask you now, with no play on words, do you have demonic possessions? If so, you need an exorcism, and you need it right now. Too bad they don't sell this kind of exorcism at the mall. No, instead they sell possessions.

Do you have a storage space for your stuff?
Since the 1970's, the number of storage spaces has increased drastically. Signs now dot the highways advertising storage spaces, and often hundreds and even thousands of these storage spaces can be seen from the highway on the outskirts of most cities and towns. This steep increase in the number of storage spaces is not a matter of more people moving and leaving their stuff in storage temporarily. To be blunt, it's yet another indication of just how much junk people have bought–so much that it no longer fits, even in very large houses.

The fact that all these possessions are in storage, where it is not convenient to make use of them on a regular basis, suggests that most of these possessions are not at all necessary. To make matters worse, it costs good money to rent a storage space. Even if a space only costs $50 per month, that's $600 per year, $6,000 in a decade. In many cases, only a few years of storage will cost more than the entire value of the contents of the storage space.

One of the strange details regarding these storage spaces is that they are referred to in advertising as "self-storage." I picture all those spaces filled with people who decided to store themselves there for a while; their lives weren't going well, and they were financially strapped, perhaps because they had stupidly bought too much stuff, so they thought the best option was to put themselves in storage. Yet because so many people confuse their stuff with their selves, perhaps this locution "self-storage" is quite accurate; people are storing what they think of as parts of themselves: self-storage, indeed.

You don't actually need all that stuff, do you?
Unless you are a truly exceptional person, you probably own a lot of stuff you don't need. You may feel that you need it. You may experience pangs of anxiety or even panic at the thought of doing without it. You may be able to provide a long list of reasons, plausible or not, why you should keep it. None of that means, however that you actually need it. The plain truth is that most of what you have you don't need, in the true sense of need.

This distinction between attachment and true need is fundamentally important. Actively distinguishing between what you truly need versus what you are merely attached to, for various reasons, can spare you later regret.

PART ONE: YOU AND YOUR STUFF

Exercise: What do you truly need?
Imagine that suddenly everything you own, absolutely everything, is lost in a natural disaster. You now have nothing but the clothes you are wearing, your abilities and skills, your qualities as a person, and your relationships. At that point, what do you truly need?

For each item you claim to need, justify in writing exactly why it is absolutely necessary. Make a list of no more than ten items, including for each item a truly convincing reason for why it is necessary. Now look at the list of no more than ten items, and prioritize the items. Now the truly hard part: shorten the list to no more than five items.

If you complete this exercise, you will have quite an experience, just imagining, and writing a little bit. You may suddenly have a deep and vivid new sense of priorities, as well as a newfound horror at the trivial in general. This one exercise, if you surrender to it completely, can permanently improve and clarify your outlook. If you keep this exercise in mind as you move through your daily life, you will find yourself easily and comfortably paying little or no attention to many of the things that, in truth, do not matter.

You are rarely, if ever, buying just one thing
I'm all in favor of bicycles, particularly if you're considering getting rid of your car. I think buying a bicycle can be an excellent choice, if done for the right reasons. Precisely because I generally would support such a purchase, I've chosen it as an example of how to think with complete clarity about all that you are buying, all the various things that you in fact are buying, when you think you're only buying one thing.

Let's say you decide you want a bicycle. You can spare the money for the bicycle, you think to yourself. A few months later, without quite knowing how it happened, you now own in addition to the bicycle a small oil can, a red flashing LED lamp, a warning bell on your handlebars, a set of bike baskets, a tire patch kit, a water bottle and water bottle clip holder, two bike pumps because the first one was a piece of junk, special gloves, a bike rack, strange shoes that you can't walk in easily, and you're standing there with your expensive bike helmet in your hand looking utterly ridiculous in your head-to-toe spandex outfit that cost you a bundle, and pushed you to the limit on your credit card. Did you buy just a bicycle?

As I said, I love bicycles, and generally support buying them. Yet every purchase is not just a purchase, but also a path that beckons you to further purchases along that path. Again, you are rarely, if ever, buying just one thing.

Exercise: What stuff of yours made you buy other stuff?
Take a few moments to analyze the causal connections among your possessions. Some possessions tend to induce you to buy many other possessions, though this may not be obvious at the early stages. Write down a few possessions that led to a large number of other possessions. For each of those few possessions, write down all the other possessions you acquired because of that first possession.

In some cases the purchase of one item leads to other items only because that first purchase is the beginning of a habit, which may harden over time. You may not buy other different items because of that first purchase, but you may buy that same item hundreds or even thousands of times after that first time.

Some examples are more severe than others, but a simple example for the sake of reference is the candy to both sides of you as you wait in line at the supermarket. Hey, you're doing nothing but waiting in line, so you take a look at the goodies. You decide to buy some gum because, well, it's only $1.69, and you're only going to buy it this one time, right? But you like the gum, so you're more ready to buy it next time. Now every time you're in the line at the supermarket, you're primed to buy the gum again, because you bought it last time. Years later, you've made hundreds and hundreds of purchases, wasted quite a hunk of money, gotten no nutritional benefit, quite possibly turned people off with your gum chewing, perhaps added to your dental bills, and generated needless gallons of saliva that you swallowed. There are many other examples like this, though cigarettes is one of the most pernicious. Can you think of others that are part of your life right now?

For one short period in my life I became accustomed to having a beer or two once in a while, a beer with a particular snap to it, a beer that reminded me of some happy times with a former girlfriend. Then I was having a beer or two more frequently. Then every dinner time it felt weird to not have a beer or two. Suddenly, I saw the path ahead; it was littered with beer bottles, and stank of stale beer. I quickly left that path, have never returned, and am glad to be free of a minor bad habit. Once in while I'll see that brand of beer in a market, and just laugh.

So watch yourself, watch for habits beginning to form. Those habits can not only become very expensive financially, but even more expensive because they push other, much better things out of your life.

PART ONE: YOU AND YOUR STUFF

The effect of your possessions on other people

Your possessions clearly affect you, in many ways, and on many levels. Yet your possessions and your relationship with your possessions also affect other people, in ways you may not be aware of, or have not thought about very much.

The most obvious example of this comes from living with a hoarder, or even visiting the house of a hoarder. Even a short visit to the house of a hoarder is a disturbing experience. In the worst cases, junk is piled to the ceiling, so heavy and so thick that you can barely maneuver inside their house. Some of it is old, yet clearly has never been used, and recently bought products are piled on top of products still in their original packaging from years ago. Many objects have been ruined from the sheer weight of all the other objects on top of them. The odor of mildew is everywhere, emanating from deep within the piles, the stacks, the layers. You immediately ask yourself "What is wrong with this person? What possesses them to buy all this? Why can't they free themselves from it?" Even very strong people can be emotionally unsettled by the experience of entering the realm of a hoarder. Your view of the person is fundamentally changed. You learned something about them you wish you didn't know. You wonder about their basic sanity. You wonder what else you don't know about them. You wonder whether you really should get to know them better, after what you've seen. You wonder how soon you can leave. You wonder how you can make sure you never have to enter their house again.

Hoarders are a particularly strong example of the effect on others of one's possessions, but there are many more examples, and the effect on others isn't just in the possessions themselves, but in the nature of the person's relationship to their possessions. I've been to social events at houses in which every detail was tasteful to an extreme, such that you felt you were at a museum in which guards were posted to make sure you didn't touch anything, and the conversation was correspondingly guarded. I've also been to houses in which there was warmth and love and welcome in every choice, in every object, and you could sit or lie down anywhere, pick up anything, and also bring up anything in conversation, all in comfort.

Have you ever been to someone's house and been creeped out by what they owned? What about the opposite? Ever visited someone and felt like you wanted to move in right away, it felt so welcoming? Have you ever been to someone's house and been creeped out by their relationship with something they owned? Again, how about the opposite? Ever visited someone and been completely charmed by their relationship with something they owned?

Now ask those questions from the perspective of others, regarding you, and your possessions. What is the effect on other people of your possessions? Do your possessions give them a sense of comfort, or discomfort? Do your possessions come across as inviting curiosity and exploration, or do they tend to send a message of restriction, of emotional shutdown? Are your possessions of a welcoming nature, or a forbidding nature? Given what you know about your relationship with your possessions, what is the effect on other people of that relationship, or rather those relationships? Does your relationship with any of your possessions get in the way of any aspect of your relationship with people?

If nothing comes to mind offhand, here are some examples:

I've been in a few homes in which I felt terrified to leave even a small fingerprint on the kitchen counter, once I witnessed the owner's obsessive cleaning.

In a few cases, the presence of many books and cultural artifacts and a clearly active relationship with those materials immediately inspired a whole set of expansive discussions, from which I learned a lot, both about the topics themselves, and about the person I was visiting.

In a few other living spaces I've visited, I quickly realized that the rooms were set up only for the comfort of those who lived there. No allowance had been made for the comfort of guests. Therefore from the choice and arrangement of furniture alone, guests felt unwelcome, and the owners were either not aware of the message they were sending, or were quite aware of that message, and didn't care.

I once knew a guy whose living quarters were deliberately constructed to be as surprising as possible. Nothing was what you expected, or where you'd expect it, or how you expected it to look. Many objects were not even easily identifiable, and were whimsically placed. You might think this would be alienating, but there was such obvious fun in all of it, that you quickly felt free to do anything, say anything–and that was exactly the intended effect. I used to love visiting there.

Ever visited someone who has a huge TV, and even as you're trying to talk with them, not only is the TV playing loudly, but they're continually glancing over to the TV, barely following the conversation? How did that make you feel? Ever been that person yourself?

Once again, take an inventory of your possessions, but this time to reflect on their effect on other people. Do you own anything that has a negative effect on people? Is the effect of your possessions on people the effect you'd like it to be? Do you accurately understand the effect of your possessions on the people in your life? What possibilities with other people are created by your possessions? What possibilities may be limited or foreclosed by your possessions?

Yet again, take an inventory of your possessions, but this time to reflect on the effect of your relationship with your possessions on your relationship with other people. Is your relationship with any of your possessions a hindrance in any way to any of your relationships? Does your relationship with any of your possessions alienate anyone, or cause resentment, or damage positive possibilities with anyone in your life? Do you notice any nearby eye-rolling when you reach once again for that...yeah, *that* thing?

The effect on you and other people of what you buy for them

Your relationship with possessions is not limited to just your possessions, but also includes anything you buy for other people. This may be gifts for relatives, friends or co-workers; items for a shared household including furniture and furnishings such as carpet and curtains, food, even down to the choice of silverware, tablecloth, the paint on the walls, and the precise choice of doormat; meals you buy for others at restaurants; any aspect of a vacation, clearly including the exact nature of the vacation itself, down to every detail. Every choice you make as to what to buy, whether a product, service or experience, when made in conjunction with other people has effects both on you and on the other people.

Buying presents for people can contain so many different qualities, attitudes and messages, anywhere from kind, generous and thoughtful to cruel, manipulative and even harmful. Many presents represent good wishes, but even good wishes can include hidden messages and unrecognized implications. Some presents are like a net covered with sharp hooks, thrown in an attempt to lash the recipient to the giver of such gifts. In certain relationships, when the emotional basis of the relationship begins to falter, the giving of "gifts" intensifies, in an effort to artificially generate good will, or obligation, or bonding. Some presents contain either overt or concealed messages. For instance, giving a person something you think they should use contains a very different message than giving them something you know would be useful to them.

Even inviting someone out to dinner "as a treat" does not always have positive implications. Many a restaurant is noisy, serves less than healthy food, and is not at all conducive to good conversation, given the inherent distractions. I've fielded invitations to dinner in restaurants were only attempts to buy my personal time by paying me with food and companionship I didn't particularly want. There are times the translation of "I'll buy you a meal" is more like "I'll waste your time and oppress you with unwanted companionship while twisting your arm and trying to make you feel obligated." A far better alternative would have been to cultivate rapport over some extent of time, then get together privately, meal or not, for meaningful conversation and exchange.

In our frenzied consumerist society, also characterized by poor understanding on an emotional level of both ourselves and others, we are encouraged to buy random gifts for people, at times as a substitute for genuine relationship or genuine understanding. If you've ever witnessed an emotionally disconnected relative shower the children in a family with gifts in the absence of genuine emotional rapport, you know the horror of which I speak. I wonder what the effect on children is in the long term of receiving at times truly excessive gifts, many of which are based in cheap, mind-numbing entertainment. Parents in particular are under pressure to buy, buy, buy for their children. But what is the effect on the children of being taught, in effect, that materialism is the primary and possibly the only concern of life?

Everything and anything you buy for another person has an effect on them, major or minor, as well as an effect on your relationship with them, on how they think of you, and on how you think of them. Every material gift, if given as a substitute for true relationship and understanding, may very well be a form of robbery, of both you and the other person. Yet the opposite is also true; there are gifts which are so full of love, and deep thought, and good wishes, which are not available in any store, nor available online. Those are also the gifts from which both people benefit.

"Retail therapy" is about as therapeutic as heroin

Once in a while I'll hear a reference to "retail therapy." Every time I hear such a reference, it comes across as apologetic, even defensive.

Most of us seem to accept, without question, that it's fine to buy things to cheer yourself up. Let's take a closer look at the implications of this claim, however.

If the only way a person can think of to lift their spirits is to go purchase an object, what does it say about the emotional and social resources in their life? What does it say about their confidence in the people in their life? What does it say about their confidence in their relationships? What does it say about their confidence in themselves and their abilities, in their understanding of themselves and their available options? What does it say about their level of creativity? What is the probable result, over a lifetime, of reinforcing the habit of trying to cheer yourself up by just going out and buying stuff?

When someone is feeling down, perhaps even feeling a bit desperate, if they respond to those feelings by implicitly giving up on any choice other than to go out and buy something, an emotional association is formed between desperation and the object purchased, between desperation and purchasing. They might be pleased with the object, but on another level the object will always remind them of the original desperation. That's not a good pattern to adopt. A second result is to degrade awareness of other options, other choices. Implicit in this is the loss of specific emotional abilities, and a loss of both imagination and self-questioning. If the habit hardens, it becomes less and less likely not only that they will try something else, but that anything else will even occur to them.

I have known people who, when they start feeling depressed, head straight to the mall. They have no confidence in their "friends." They have no confidence in themselves. They just buy lots of stuff, and often end up later hating both themselves and the stuff they bought. Life itself is cheapened, even as the interest on the credit card balance gets more expensive.

"Retail therapy," often mentioned with a defensive chuckle, is about as therapeutic as heroin. The final results can be quite similar.

Blindly accepting the injection of alien desires is not a dignified way to live

Does that sound gross? The reality is much more disgusting. What do I mean by "the injection of alien desires?" Consider how many of the things you now own were the result of your unconsciously being convinced by the forces of peer pressure, conformity, and marketing that you needed them, when in fact you didn't need them at all? What you may have experienced as a desire for a particular object was actually a desire that was cleverly injected into you. It wasn't actually your desire, but a desire by someone or something else for you to desire the object. The desire was originally alien to you. The desire was injected into you. You were also likely convinced, through a subtle process, that the decision was actually yours, that you chose the object freely, even though you didn't. Below is an example.

At breakfast among several people at a B&B in New Lebanon, New York recently, talked turned to the state of the world. The usual complaints ensued, not worth mention here. You know what they are. I made the point that much of the problem actually is that most of us are part of a vast structure of conformity, and that most of us only do what most other people do, think what most other people think, and that many of us don't even realize that what we experience as our own desires are not our own desires at all, but have been determined by the system, and implanted in us.

One person become noticeably agitated by what I had just said, and suddenly piped up, his voice rising above a normal level, declaring strongly that all his desires were absolutely his own, and that he was absolutely doing his own thing. Swiftly he cited all his "toys," as he called them—his cars, his motorcycle, his boat, his electronic gadgets. There wasn't a single non-cliché in the list. He asserted very strongly again that he was absolutely doing his own thing. He went on to say that he'd be bored to death without his "toys." In other words, he would have no idea what to do with himself in the absence of all the things he had been convinced to want, and therefore to buy, and yet he was stirred to fury by the suggestion that he wasn't truly his own man.

That's not a dignified way to live. There is a much more dignified way to live, based on noble values.

Conclusion of Part One
Obviously, the degree to which you change your relationship with your possessions, as well as whether you do so at all, is entirely up to you. You may decide that you are completely happy with everything you own, how and why you got it, and happy with your relationship with all of it. If so, that's great. By some amazing miracle you managed to escape the influence of our entire society, were never subject to peer pressure of any kind in any way, have never been influenced to the slightest degree by marketing, have only beautiful and admirable

PART ONE: YOU AND YOUR STUFF

motivations, and have deep and abiding noble values and nothing but noble values which you adhere to without exception, particularly as expressed in your meticulous adherence to those values in every one of your purchases throughout your life. However, if there's still doubt about whether you fit that description, please read further.

"The sweet things in life to you were just loaned
So how can you lose what you never owned?"

– Life Is Just A Bowl of Cherries

TRANSITION: A NEW RELATIONSHIP WITH STUFF

If you got all the way through Part One, you now have a much better understanding of your relationship with your stuff. You may have been surprised by some of the questions raised so far and, if you completed the exercises, may also have been surprised by some of your own answers. So now that you've taken stock of your relationship with your possessions, you may be inclined to unburden yourself of some of them. If you are now motivated to reduce the burden of your possessions, I encourage you to do so not in a sudden fit of purging, but in a gradual, thoughtful and responsible way.

Let's quickly examine some of the advantages of having fewer possessions, consider ways of responsibly unburdening yourself of unwanted or unnecessary possessions, and consider how to become much more thoughtful about acquiring any new possessions.

Advantages of having less stuff

The advantages to having less stuff are many and various. While some of the reasons are obvious, awareness of those reasons is often suppressed by the incessant drumbeat of marketing in all its forms that surrounds us, the pressure to conform, and our habits formed over a lifetime as a result of this. Therefore it would be helpful to review all the reasons explicitly, one by one, as to why having less stuff can be an ongoing positive factor in your life.

Save money: Reason 1

An obvious reason to have less stuff is so that you didn't spend, or in many cases waste good money buying that stuff in the first place. Financial freedom depends on having room to maneuver, in financial matters. The majority of purchases limit your financial freedom, though the effect is most often piecemeal; each individual purchase just takes a small bite out of your financial freedom, but all those little bites can eventually leave nothing left for major choices you may want to make. Would you trade away truly valuable major new possibilities in your life for a pile of petty possessions? Well, then don't.

Save money: Reason 2

Having stuff often means taking care of your stuff, and this can cost money as well, in some cases a lot of money. Many homeowners discover this the hard way; you may think you're buying a house, but you're actually buying a huge obligation of maintenance, taxes, and "improvements," over the course of many years. Maintenance of a car can in some cases exceed the cost of the car itself, not even counting all the insurance paid over the course of years. The same goes for lots of other possessions. You can avoid all those costs of maintenance by not making those purchases in the first place.

Save money: Reason 3
This point was made previously, but the third reason to have less stuff is so that you're not even tempted to buy stuff to go with your other stuff. Stuff begets more stuff, and stuff always costs you, so keep your financial freedom by reducing the rate of proliferation of your stuff as close to zero as you can.

Save time
Some stuff saves you time, it's true. Yet other stuff can cost you time, in some cases lots of time. It's a good idea to develop the habit of actively evaluating everything you own, and noticing what takes your time, but does not provide a genuine benefit worth the time.

With some possessions we may feel an obligation to make use of whatever it is, only because we paid for it. That's a mistake. It would be better to ask, "Should I have even bought this in the first place?" The answer to that question may make us wince with regret, but it's better to get the wincing over with and learn a good lesson than waste time trying in vain to justify a bad decision. Regularly asking yourself whether you should have bought certain possessions in the first place can also help a great deal in preventing bad decisions, regret and waste of time in the future, because you'll be training yourself to make better decisions.

More room for what actually matters
There are many ways your stuff can interfere with other aspects of your life that are more important. When you have less stuff however, you also have less to think about that doesn't really matter, so it's easier to think about what truly does matter. Having less stuff also reduces the amount of attention you pay, and therefore lose, in considering what other stuff to get to go with your stuff.

There is also a directly practical aspect to having less stuff, and a literal aspect of "more room for what actually matters." Stuff takes up space, often space that could be better used. One of the best uses of physical space is for new possibilities. I've visited many a house in which new possibilities were squeezed out by an excess of stuff.

Sometimes that meant a "guest room" that couldn't be used for guests because it was full of junk. No guests means no extended social visits, no nice breakfast together in the morning, no interesting discoveries through spending extended time together in genuine hospitality. All of that would be lost, just for a room full of junk. So make the room, and keep the room, for what matters most, physically, mentally and emotionally.

Greater mental and emotional clarity
In many ways, your stuff can clog your mind, and can clog the flow of your emotions. If you've ever gone backpacking or on an extended trip or otherwise experienced temporary complete freedom from nearly all your possessions, you may have been astounded by how clear your mind became within only a few days. Clearing your life of unnecessary possessions can have the same effect, but on an ongoing basis, every single day. That's worth a whole lot more than a pile of junk.

Less guilt, more valid self-esteem
Many of the things we've bought are not at all a source of pride. I've bought quite a few things that made me feel ashamed before I even left the store. There's no point keeping anything you regret buying, but the most important skill to learn is to buy only what you know you will be proud to have bought. Less guilt about being an idiot for buying all that stuff means more valid self-esteem, more energy, and better possibilities in your life.

For every item, keep in mind the advantages of not owning it
Because our entire society is structured to convince you that there are only advantages to owning absolutely anything and everything, it can be a challenge to keep in mind that for any given item, there are also advantages to not owning it, not to mention disadvantages to owning it. Many of the advantages of non-ownership are of fundamental importance, and become obvious with only a bit of thought, but this requires effort in order to counteract the hypnotic claims of advertising combined with social influences.

For many people, a car is considered a necessity, even if in fact it is not a necessity, but merely considered one. Even if a car is considered a necessity, the advantages to not owning one remain valid. Yet rarely are the numerous advantages of not owning a car mentioned, or even discussed. It's as though there is a taboo about discussing the advantages of not owning this central icon of mindless materialism. Let's break that taboo right now, and do so comprehensively.

Advantages of not owning a car:

1. Save money by not buying it in the first place
2. Save money by not paying insurance year after year
3. Save money by not paying for gasoline time after time
4. Save money by never having to pay for maintenance or repairs
5. Save your life by avoiding car accidents
6. Spend less time under the bad influence of traffic
7. Get more done by spending less time in the car
8. Improve your health by walking more
9. No more washing your car, when you don't have one
10. No one will judge your car, when you don't have one
11. You won't be tempted to buy additional accessories for a car you don't have
12. You'll never be disappointed by the inevitable deterioration of a car you don't have
13. You won't be tempted to listen to the hideous radio stations in the car when you don't have one
14. You may discover an entire world of experience that is much more humane, much more interesting, and much more inspiring
15. Your mood and attitude may improve

This list is not complete, in part because each person may perceive advantages to not owning a car that are unique to their outlook, their experience, and their circumstances. Can you think of advantages to not owning a car that were not included in the list above?

Let's immediately move on to breaking the same taboo, but concerning a few other items currently considered "necessities." Observe that the pattern is the same as with cars; there is a pretense that ownership is always and in every way desirable, as well as a pretense that there are no advantages to not owning the item. For each of the items listed below, think of every advantage to not owning the item:

TRANSITION: A NEW RELATIONSHIP WITH STUFF

1. A house
2. A television
3. A computer
4. A cell phone

    You should have been able to list several advantages to non-ownership for each item. You may have been surprised by the strength and significance of some of those advantages, as well as by how obvious the advantages are once you begin to think of them. I encourage you to universalize this practice; for anything you are considering buying, consciously enumerate the advantages of not buying it. Society will automatically take care of aggressively inserting into your mind the supposed advantages of buying the item. It's up to you, however to supply the counterargument–in case after case after case. This is the only way to achieve true freedom of choice in your purchases.

    As a further example of true freedom of choice, consider that for each of the items listed above, and indeed for everything you ever consider owning, the exact characteristics of the item, as well as how you use it, as well as the precise nature of the relationship you have with the item, are entirely up to you. Evaluate for yourself, according to your own independent judgment, the assumptions commonly attached to all possessions, and potential possessions. Such assumptions are omnipresent, but can be difficult to discern, precisely because they are undeclared, unconscious assumptions, and because their recognition as assumptions is discouraged by society.

    For instance, a particularly bizarre, frequently destructive yet generally unquestioned assumption is attached to the ownership of a house. You may have heard the advice "Buy the biggest house you can afford." Accompanying this advice is the implication that if you don't do so, you may be crazy, and possibly downright un-American, but in any case a pathetic loser. But examine the implications of this advice for a moment. Why exactly should someone buy a house bigger than they need, bigger than they want, or bigger than would be convenient for them?

    Buying a house that is truly tiny is a perfectly valid choice, if that's what you want to do, as is buying a house with any particular set of characteristics, no matter what those characteristics are, if that's what you want.

    You can apply this same principle to any possession, any object. Buying a used, ancient television that doesn't even work and then converting it into a fish tank or a lumber box or a lighted display case for your collection of scarab beetles or copies of Mad Magazine or plastic Japanese artificial food samples is also a valid choice, as is buying a cell phone and then only turning it on when you need to make an outgoing call in an emergency, while never allowing the cell phone and its possible intrusions to rule your mind.

Just because everyone else uses something a particular way doesn't mean you have to use it that way. You can use anything you want, any way you want.

Owning it doesn't mean you have to keep it

Once we own something, we may have mixed feelings about getting rid of it. Sometimes the mentality of "I paid good money for this, so I'm going to keep it no matter what" kicks in. Sometimes you keep the item because even thinking about getting rid of it forces you to confront the fact that you probably shouldn't have bought it anyway, and that can be embarrassing, so you avoid even thinking about getting rid of it just to avoid feeling like a fool. Sometimes a possession can become so much a part of our daily habits that it becomes part of our identity, even when we see it's bad for us. For some people, the idea of parting with anything at all fills them with a nameless terror.

Yet in all cases the truth is that owning something does not mean you have to keep it. After all, you once didn't own it, and didn't own it for all the previous years of your life, and you were just fine. You'll be just fine once it's gone too, and in the process you'll have an opportunity to make better choices as to how to spend your money, time and attention. If something became part of your identity, when you part with it you have a new chance at a better identity.

If you haven't used it in a year, get rid of it

This simple guideline has worked well for me. I once had a lot of stuff that I didn't use very much. When I first heard of this guideline, I began reflecting on how long it had been since I had made use of certain possessions. In some cases, I was shocked at how long it had been. Some of those possessions would have been very helpful to other people, so I felt bad about keeping things I clearly didn't need, when others might actually need them.

It is obvious that this guideline does not apply to certain possessions. Some possessions are not a matter of utility, but of meaning. It makes no sense to ask when you last "used" precious pictures from your childhood, for instance. But an elaborate Cuisinart that you used once when you first bought it five years ago, and never used again? Exercise equipment that you used for about two weeks seven years ago, and has been rusting in your garage ever since? A stack of magazines you've been swearing for the past five years you'll eventually start reading, even though you know you actually won't?

A simple trick for keeping track of when you last used certain possessions is to put a small sticker on whatever the object is, with the date you last used it. Periodically review these stickers. You may be in for a new form of "sticker shock" as you discover how infrequently you use certain things. If you haven't used something in a long time, certainly if you haven't used it in several years, please consider selling it or giving it away. You'll probably be glad if you do, and if you devise a way to both rid yourself of the object and provide a benefit to someone else, you'll be making more than one person happy.

Excellent ways to get rid of stuff

There are truly excellent ways to get rid of stuff, ways that benefit both you and other people, with little or no inconvenience, and even some benefits you may not have thought of. You can even make the process fun, interesting, and a guarantee of both positive connections with other people and pride in the result.

Donate to a women's shelter

A truly excellent way to get rid of unwanted possessions is to locate a women's shelter in your area which accepts donations. You'll be helping women in need, and often helping children affected by difficult situations as well. I once donated more than half of my possessions to a women's shelter in San Francisco, including an expensive bicycle and other valuable items. Making that large donation was one of the best decisions I've ever made, and is still a source of pride, many years on.

Schedule a non-profit pickup

In many communities it's now very easy to either schedule a pickup, or find out when the next pickup is already scheduled. Large organizations such as the Salvation Army have web sites on which you can schedule a pickup. In most cases you will have to specify what you are offering, and some items may not be accepted. For instance, you should not expect any organization to come out and pick up your beat up old couch that no one would want. But other furniture in reasonable condition will probably be accepted, and many other items as well.

Donate to a thrift store
Nearly every community of significant size has at least one thrift store, and often more. Goodwill is not the only game in town, and sometimes Goodwill does not accept certain items that will be accepted by other thrift stores. I strongly recommend making a list of at least three thrift stores, checking their hours, then mapping a route to stop by all three of them. Thrift stores tend to occur in clusters, so usually it's easy to stop by a few stores that are close to each other. If certain items are not accepted at the first one, move on to the second and give it a try, and so on.

Hold a garage sale
A garage sale isn't just a way of getting rid of stuff. It's a way of getting some cash for your excess belongings, and it's a social event. Just be sure to be a good neighbor by putting a date on any signs you put up, and take all the signs down when your garage sale is over. One word of warning about inviting lots of people you know to your garage sale; you may be inviting trouble, if any of these people get a case of buyer's remorse, or are later dissatisfied with what they bought from you. Hearing from friends at length and in detail about the stuff they bought from you is not a good use of your time, and has the potential to damage relationships. It's probably better to just put up a set of signs, and deal with whoever comes by, with a "no returns" policy prominently posted.

Sell on eBay or hire an eBay seller
Depending on what you own, you may be able to sell some of your stuff on eBay. Selling on eBay is some people's idea of a good time, but it's sure not mine. If you enjoy it, that's great, but there are now services that will come by and pick up items that can be sold on eBay, and sell them for you. Obviously you won't make as much money as you would if you sold them yourself, but you won't be wasting your time, either.

Schedule a commercial pickup
There are services that will come by in a large truck to haul away your junk, and some of them accept really big junk. The most famous and largest is 1-800-GOT-JUNK. The good news is they'll take lots and lots

of different kinds of junk. The bad news is that you'll have to pay them to take it away. But that might be better than your either hauling your junk to a landfill and paying the landfill yourself, or your continuing to hold on to your junk. The other good news is that these services are tied in to appliance repair and recycling companies, so at least some of your junk will be put to good secondary use.

Donate to an e-waste recycler
It's easier and easier to find e-waste recyclers, and some of them will take your old equipment for free. Just get on the web and locate the ones near you and find out what they take, and on what terms. Please don't just throw your old electronic equipment in the dumpster. That's a waste of the precious materials in the equipment, and terrible for the environment.

Locate a hazmat dropoff
If you have stuff like car batteries, old paint and pesticides or other chemicals, it's important to dispose of these items responsibly. Locate a hazmat center in your area, and find out their hours and procedures. You're being a good citizen, but be prepared for a possibly spooky experience at the facility. They have to deal with all kinds of dangerous material, and they usually don't know what will be arriving in any given load. When I dropped off a few cans of paint, I was instructed by a guy in a full hazmat suit to drive up to a yellow line and no further, and to stay in my car while he removed the items from the trunk. I then had to present my complete id, and sign a form certifying exactly what I had dropped off. They keep track of who drops off what, so that you can't just set up a business disposing of large amounts of dangerous material. Hazardous old stuff in your home? Take a nice little field trip to your friendly neighborhood hazmat dropoff.

Make your riddance truly good
If you've gone through the experience of riddance, I hope it was good. Riddance can be a wonderful, liberating, enlightening experience. Sometimes it takes more than just one cycle, though. I had to go through three large cycles of acquisition followed by purging before finally reaching an equilibrium in which I am completely happy with what I have, use it all well, and no longer have the slightest buyer's remorse when I do buy something, because I've trained myself to be

much more thoughtful whenever I consider buying anything. I now no longer ever need to purge, because I never accumulate questionable possessions.

Advantages of buying less stuff

Sorry to repeat this point, but many people still don't seem to have it straight that buying stuff means your money goes away; they keep buying loads and loads of products, then are puzzled why their money's tight. Could it possibly be because of all the things they bought?

Once you get in the habit of buying less stuff, and are fully confident that you are no longer subject to the urge to buy stuff you don't actually need, additional benefits accrue. When you are no longer spending time shopping, you also aren't spending time thinking about shopping, or planning shopping. You can now turn more of your attention to making more significant choices for yourself and your life.

One of the greatest advantages of buying less stuff is that you are no longer behaving like a mindless robot. You can take pride in this, and enjoy the exercise of your new freedom. Becoming less of a robot programmed by your society may also bring with it an expanded perspective, and a surge in your own creativity. Here's hoping that's the case for you.

Choose any new stuff thoughtfully and carefully

We all need to buy stuff on occasion, but most of us are not truly thoughtful about what we do buy. As you consider any new purchases, think about exactly what you've learned in the process of evaluating your relationship with your stuff, and in the process of ridding yourself of unneeded possessions. In the following few pages, let's review the advantages of buying less stuff, consider how to evaluate possible future purchases, and do a couple of exercises in order to maintain perspective on all that damn stuff out there that your entire society is trying to convince you to buy.

You will always need stuff, but if you've gotten this far in the book your awareness of how little you actually need has probably deepened. You may already have your own ideas about changing the way you go about acquiring new possessions. If you've had much experience with "buyer's remorse," you may have already been motivated to think carefully about exactly why you made purchases you later regretted, and you may have already made adjustments in the way you think about possible new purchases.

I used to be very sloppy in what I chose to buy, and I've had some harsh experiences with buyer's remorse, so I made major adjustments in how I went about even considering buying anything at all. I now have an internal psychological checklist I use, that goes something like this:

- Do I actually need this thing, or do I just feel that I need it?
- Why, exactly why, do I want this thing at all?
- If I stopped thinking about it for a couple of weeks, would I still want it?
- Am I lying to myself in some way about why I want it, in order not to feel embarrassed about why I actually want it?
- Given that most purchases have an emotional basis, can I satisfy the underlying emotional desire in some way that doesn't involve buying anything at all?
- Am I completely confident that, a year from now or five years from now, I will still like this thing and be glad I bought it?
- What am I giving up, in money, time, and possible other opportunities if I buy this thing?
- What effect will this thing probably have on me?
- Will this thing probably have a good effect, or a bad effect, on other areas of my life, such as relationships?

I encourage you to develop your own internal checklist as you consider any purchases. Do not confine use of this checklist only to big-ticket items, because your buying behavior is a cluster of habits, and if you don't practice on the smaller things, you probably won't be good at dealing with the bigger things, either. Once you get used to going through your internal checklist, you will be do so in a matter of only a few seconds, so it's not a burden, but the benefit is enormous.

Exercise: Develop and use an internal checklist for purchases
Write down questions you think would be helpful to you in making positive changes to how you approach buying things. Try to put the questions in the best sequence possible. The next time you want to buy something, particularly if it's something in a category in which you've previously had some buyer's remorse (Clothing? Furniture?

Computers? Kitchen gadgets? New car?), get out your checklist and go through every question, applying it to the thing you want to buy. This should be a very illuminating process. Do this a few times until you can do it without looking at the checklist.

Exercise: Strongly skeptical window shopping
Embark on this exercise only once you feel completely secure and stable in your outlook toward new purchases. If you still feel weak and controlled by urges toward making senseless purchases, do more work on this until you have achieved greater understanding of yourself and your motivations, and are no longer subject to such urges. If you try this exercise before you are truly ready, it may backfire, so be completely honest with yourself about whether you are truly in control of yourself. Don't try this exercise until you're sure you're ready.

Version 1: Take all the money out of your wallet, and remove all the credit cards. Keep your ID in your wallet, but no means to buy anything.

Version 2: Leave everything in your wallet, including cash and credit cards, just as normal. This is the more difficult version, for some people.

Head out for some high-performance window shopping. This means hitting some of your favorite retail outlets, but with seriously enhanced self-awareness, seriously enhanced awareness of the environment you will be placing yourself in, and full understanding of your mission. That mission consists of four goals:

1. *Don't buy anything at all.*
2. *Study the environment carefully, from a critical distance.*
3. *Observe your responses, and changes of state.*
4. *Return home having learned a lot, and proud of having done so.*

Exercise: Isn't it ridiculous?
This exercise is a variation on the above exercise, but with the serious addition of a humorous critical perspective. This time, embark on your high-performance window shopping as above, but now your goal is specifically to observe how utterly ridiculous every aspect of the retail

environment is, and to probe the absurdity of its additional related aspects.

Head out once more into the weird, warped world of retail. It's best to go to a large mall, but nearly any cluster of retail outlets will do, and you can even get precisely the same effect by visiting any supermarket, or even a small store of nearly any kind.

Pretend you are either an alien visiting Earth, or a time traveller from 1,000 years ago. Either choice will do just fine, and have the same effect. Now take a look at what is being offered for sale, as though you've never seen any of it before, and need to be informed as to what it is exactly, and why people think they need it, or think they should want it. Sink into the experience.

If most of what is for sale begins to look truly bizarre, outlandish, utterly idiotic or clearly destructive, you're on the right track. If there are advertisements or promotions in the environment, study them also as though you have never seen anything like them before. Observe the images that are used to accompany the products. Observe the language and the images that are used. Observe the multiple levels of attempted emotional and social manipulation in these materials, when the products themselves are for the most part completely unnecessary and in many cases garish, unhealthy, wasteful, personally degrading and ridiculous.

Now take this all one vast step further. Imagine what was required to design, build, transport and market all these products. Imagine all the people who had many meetings to plan all aspects of the products, again and again, for hours at a time, over the course of months and years. Imagine the careful selection of an advertising agency, just to convince people to buy the products. Imagine the lengthy discussions of the precise choices within the elaborate marketing campaign for the products. Imagine all the people within all the companies studying their competitors' products, in order to gain advantages in selling their own products.

If you return home feeling as though you've visited a planet dominated by bizarre creatures who have no realistic sense of their own actual needs, no perspective on their own behavior, and little or no relation to deeper values of any kind, you have now completed your mission to the planet Earth in the 21st century. Whether as an alien or as a time traveller from long ago, you now have a glimpse of our zombie-infested planet.

Every desire is actually a desire for a feeling
With the exception of primary needs such as breathing and eating, which are necessary for us to stay alive, nearly all other "needs" are actually only desires, though some may be very strong. Every desire, though more often than not attached psychologically to specific objects, people, or conditions, is ultimately only a desire for a feeling. You may think you want that car, but the underlying truth is that you want particular feelings you have come to associate with that car. You may think you have a burning desire for that new gadget, but really you are just in the grip of desire for feelings you think that gadget will provide. You may think it's those supposedly fabulous new clothes you want, but really you just want to feel a certain way, and you think those clothes will help you feel that way.

Gaining a clear understanding that every desire is only a desire for a feeling is of crucial importance in safely and sanely navigating the oceans of pretense and deception of your society. For instance, some ways of satisfying a desire for a feeling or emotional state are not damaging in any way, have no disadvantages, and lead to good results over the long term. Other ways of trying to satisfy a desire are inherently damaging, involve numerous disadvantages, and can lead to disaster in the long term.

Consider the example of people who, in the pursuit of what they consider high status, go into deep and unmanageable debt, ruin their relationships and the deeper opportunities of life, and ultimately come to despise themselves. Along the way, they thought they wanted that huge house, that extravagant car, those expensive furnishings to fill that huge house, and all those pricey gifts they used in a lame attempt to show off. But what did they really want, at the most fundamental level? They wanted to feel good about themselves. At the end of it all, they damaged their own lives, and ended up hating themselves. Did they get what they wanted? No, not at all. They got the opposite of what they wanted. Why? Because they failed to recognize their actual, underlying desire, and so failed to satisfy that desire in a healthy, reasonable and flexible set of ways.

It is of course quite natural to want to feel good about yourself. We all want to feel good about ourselves. There is an immense difference, however between linking your feelings of self-worth to belongings or symbols of status, and linking your feelings of self-worth to qualities and abilities you have worked to achieve. The first linkage is shallow, unstable and depends on the fickle attention of other people. The second linkage is deep, stable and truly your own, for your entire life.

In a similar way, you could link your desire for emotional and mental stimulation to purchases of products, and spend lots of money accumulating possessions which you then have to house, manage and maintain. In the case of the desire for emotional and mental stimulation, the possessions purchased in trying to satisfy this desire often lose their effectiveness quickly. If you've ever bought something thinking it would bring great stimulation to your life only to find that a few months later you can't stand to look at it because it seems so boring or so limited, you know exactly what I mean.

A much better approach to satisfying your desire for emotional and mental stimulation is to deliberately choose ways of changing your self, and changing your life, so that the stimulation you need is always present, or within easy reach. Even better is to deliberately choose types of stimulation that tend to lead to new opportunities of many different kinds, and further stimulation. In my own life, I deliberately seek out people who have interesting ideas, and interesting areas of knowledge, who have deep curiosity, and who are excellent conversationalists. Many times my conversations with these people lead directly to wonderful new opportunities, at a cost of exactly zero dollars, and with great pleasure in the conversations themselves.

Whether the desire is for safety, pride, social belonging, emotional or mental stimulation, or just deep contentment, the desire can be fulfilled in many ways. Society will always try to fool you into believing that your desires can only be satisfied through purchase of a product or service. Throw off that spell. Reject the false messages. Learn to understand the underlying nature of your desires, and then evaluate ways of satisfying those desires. Become creative and flexible in satisfying your desires, and give preference to those ways that lead to further advantages, cost nothing, benefit others as well as yourself, and further develop you as a person.

In other words, embrace noble values, instead of just stuff.

PART TWO: DEEPER VALUES

"Life is about more than just maintaining oneself, it is about extending oneself. Otherwise living is only not dying."

— Simone de Beauvoir (1908-1986)

For most of the book up to this point, we've dealt with many of the issues involved in living a life oriented toward possessions, acquisition, and unquestioning consumerist conformity. From here to the end of the book, we will examine a much better, much deeper, far more interesting and far more satisfying approach to life: the choice to live in relation to noble values.

Below is the list of fundamental values on which the remainder of this book is based. Your own values may differ in some ways. Perhaps you haven't yet done the work of clearly defining, questioning, revising and refining your values. Whatever may be the case for you, I invite you to evaluate and critique the values which have become the foundation of my life, and consider whether in your opinion these values are worthy. If so, please adopt them yourself, go about living in relation to them in your own way. My values:

- Honesty, above all with oneself, despite the discomfort that may be involved.

- Ongoing development as a person, based in the exercise of honesty.

- Creativity, based in one's development as a person.

- True dignity, through valid self-improvement.

- Concern for the quality of our life together, in every way.

- Full and complete acceptance of responsibility for the quality of the choices we make, great and small, and the effect of those choices on other people.

- Good citizenship, on every level: neighborhood, local area, region, state, country, collection of nations, our small and irreplaceable planet.

These values are not at all the values of our society. In all probability society will never have noble values, but will always be stuck in the muck of senseless, mindless, spiritless "thingism," unconscious destructive reactivity, unacknowledged ugly motives, and systemic dishonesty about all of this and more. I would strongly advise you never to waste a moment of your time hoping that society in general will improve to include noble values. Chances are, it will not. Look to yourself instead. Look to what you can do. Look to clarifying further your own values, and how to best live by those values.

Adopting values that are contrary to your society will inevitably create a degree of tension in your relationship with society. Since the people you know are all members of your society, some of them may react to evidence of your differing values in ways that represent an effort at "enforcement" of prevailing norms. In nearly all cases the person acting to enforce prevailing norms will have no idea that this is what they are doing. The experience of being mocked or disdained by someone who is only unconsciously enforcing societal norms can be both unpleasant, and deeply disappointing. Please don't take such an experience personally, but only try to understand it.

Most people will be politely puzzled if you take strong action to alter your relationship with possessions. There will be others who will fully support you, and you may find that you develop very strong bonds with the people who do support you, based on shared values. You may also find some of your relationships shifting, or your level of interest in various relationships and social connections changing, depending on how people respond. That's all to be expected.

Transition toward deeper values

For some people, the transition to a life based on deeper values and self-improvement instead of "thingism" can be disorienting. The transition involves three aspects: inward experiences, outward changes, and outward reactions by others to those changes. Let's address the inward changes first.

If you completed the exercise of imagining yourself as an alien visiting Earth in the 21st century, or as a time traveller from a millennium ago, you probably feel a bit strange now. Many of the objects you encounter, even though you had seen them many times before, may now appear silly, strange, destructive, petty or idiotic. If you still own a television, commercials for products may now appear as inane and insane as they actually are. You are not mistaken in these

PART TWO: DEEPER VALUES

perceptions. As you think more deeply about all of this, you may experience a deep disillusionment and disappointment with your society. Do not be at all surprised by this. In so many ways, your society does not deserve much respect. In some ways it does, but in many ways it absolutely does not.

You may even reach a point at which you despise major aspects of your society. Anyone with an active sense of justice and dignity who develops an accurate view of their own society reaches this point. Many people have this experience, so you are not alone–far from it. Yet you may feel very alone, alienated, wondering how you fit in and even whether you want to fit in. You may also struggle to define your own personal values on a basis independent of society. There you are, surrounded by society, reliant on society, yet objecting to major aspects of society. What to do?

In addition to all this, you may experience social interaction in a new way, and find yourself noticing aspects of others' behavior you had never noticed before. For instance, you may notice that certain people in your life are strongly oriented toward possessions, and oriented toward activities that always involve possessions or always involve spending money. You may also notice that many of these activities are rigidly conformist. After all, going to a sports event or a movie or a concert or out to dinner aren't exactly deeply original ideas.

You may be newly puzzled as to how to spend your time, and this can also be very uncomfortable. If you've rid yourself of a lot of possessions, your patterns of attention and use of time may be strongly disrupted. If you have experienced any of this disorientation or confusion, please recognize and give yourself credit for doing something brave, rare and admirable. Very few people are able to free themselves from the matrix of consumerist conformity in their society. Most of all, just keep going on in the journey.

You will also almost certainly feel the pull of old habits. That's normal, of course. If you are experiencing heightened awareness, and that awareness is uncomfortable or tiring, you may find yourself yearning for "the dumb old days." That's also completely normal. The most important thing you can do is to maintain a sense of excitement about creating a new and much better set of choices about how to spend your precious time, attention and energy.

The next level of the transition involves outward changes, primarily in your own behavior. These changes can occur in all different aspects of your behavior, from large changes in how you spend your time, to who you choose to spend it with, what you choose to do when you're with them, right down to subtleties in your manner, timing, in the tone of your voice and the expressions on your face. You may even look different to other people. A person whose mind is full of a questioning awareness and a creative attitude toward their own behavior looks distinctly different from someone who is locked in the unawareness induced by habit and social conformity. It's possible some people will even comment on your manner or behavior, either positively, negatively or just inquiringly.

This leads us to the third aspect of the transition, that of the reactions of others to the changes they detect in you. If it's quite obvious that you're changing, this is bound to trigger stronger reactions, and often the strongest reactions are from the people closest to you, or supposedly closest to you. Be prepared. Some of the reactions may be unpleasant.

If people in your life know specifically that you are actively changing your view of possessions, and relationship with possessions, some of those people will become defensive, and this defensiveness will show up in all different forms, anything from subtle or not so subtle avoidance to sarcastic comments to sudden blurting about how they don't think you should be judging them, even if you're not judging them. Some people may even put pressure on you in different ways to halt the process of change, and return to your previous state, and views, and behavior.

It's crucial to maintain your own perspective in all of this. If you notice someone reacting to how you are changing, try to determine the emotional cause of their reaction. Is it just because they're not sure where they stand with you now, so they're nervous? Do they feel implicitly judged and therefore resentful? Are they just conformists who are putting pressure on you to get back in line? Are they genuinely concerned about you and just don't understand what you're doing? Try to be as accurate as you can in discerning the underlying emotional reasons for their responses, and don't take any of it personally. This is your own individual journey as a person. If others eventually like the results you create in your own life, they can make their own choices based on what they see.

Let's move on now to specific, positive ways of relating to new possessions, appreciating the material world and all its wonders, and beginning to relate more strongly to the less visible yet equally important world of the mind, the spirit, individual character and personal capabilities.

PART TWO: DEEPER VALUES

Develop and deepen your relationship with truth

Most people have either a lax relationship with truth, or an adversarial, self-mendacious relationship with truth. Put another way, most people either don't care much about truth, or are actively lying to themselves in order to avoid it. Neither of those attitudes or responses toward truth is admirable, but more important is that neither is productive. A deep and positive relationship with and responses toward truth contain a power, a creative power of productive transformation, far beyond what most people even consider possible. Developing and deepening your relationship with the process of truth, and truth is actually a process, is absolutely fundamental for further development as a human being. There is no genuine integrity without such a relationship. There is no possibility of genuine self-knowledge without such a relationship. There is no escape from the prison of the ego without such a relationship.

In order to present the next set of ideas with complete clarity, I must first present a definition of truth which is more accurate and more comprehensive than that in common use.

First, truth is not a static condition. Truth is not just a set of "facts." Truth is a process of discovery, limited by our nature as human beings, as well as limited in specific ways by our individual nature. Truth for all human beings is always incomplete, because no person is of infinite capability or infinite capacity, and no person has perfect judgment. Thus the emphasis should be on continuing the process of discovery without limit: there is always more to discover, more to absorb, more ways to improve one's judgment, more ways to expand one's awareness.

For most of us, certain kinds of truth, or truth about certain aspects of our lives, is something we are careful to keep at bay. In fact, we are so adept at avoiding certain realizations, so accurate in our avoidance and prevention of certain realizations, that we must on some level already understand unconsciously what we don't want to understand consciously, or we wouldn't be so skilled at preventing conscious realization. This unconscious avoidance can go on for a very long time, in many cases indefinitely, and can take many forms. Thus truth never "arrives," but is always present and available. All that happens in a deep realization is that, for whatever reason or reasons, at a particular time we are finally ready to accept a little bit more truth, or perhaps suddenly a lot more truth. In many cases, once we have consciously recognized more truth about a situation, another person, or ourselves, we are amazed that we didn't recognize it sooner. All the signs are suddenly clear, and sometimes we are embarrassed not to have been able to recognize them much earlier. "Why didn't I see all this before?" We've all had that experience.

So how can we become more skilled at recognizing and accepting truth, how can we quicken the process of conscious recognition of truth we encounter? One way is to become adept at recognizing the signs of an encounter with truth, which often are only the signs of our own resistance.

Signs of an encounter with truth
Truth exists in an infinite range of forms, so encounters with truth also occur in an infinite range of forms. Sometimes an encounter with truth takes the form of ecstasy, at other times the form of misery, or shame, or a pure and beautiful curiosity, or a tranquil and gradual realization, or a sudden, fiery explosion of insight. Contrary to the popular saying, truth doesn't always hurt, and many things other than truth or opposed to truth or the opposite of truth hurt terribly. So pain is not necessarily a reliable indicator of an encounter with truth. In my experience, there are only two consistent signs of a successful encounter with truth:

1. You are surprised in some way, on some level.
2. You are changed in ways over which you have no control.

Given that truth is always available in infinite amounts at all times, it is primarily our resistance which determines how much truth we accept and absorb. If you do want to have a deeper relationship with truth, it's crucial to become a serious student of your own resistance. Resistance is a crafty trickster, able to fool us in many ways: making us unable to see what is right in front of us; generating interpretations which prevent us from having important realizations; making us forget what we realized only the day before, or week before, or minute before; creating distractions to prevent us from paying attention to important information; making our self-contradictions appear not to be self-contradictory at all, at least to us.

Once you begin to pay attention to your own resistance, you will begin to see patterns. Each of us has our own set of methods of resistance, our own habits of resistance, such that our resistance as individuals tends to take particular forms. For some people, distractions are the preferred method. For others, it is waves of vagueness; just as a realization begins to take shape, the mind becomes terribly vague, causing the potential realization to dissipate.

For some, it is out and out avoidance, accompanied by specious claims to justify the avoidance. At times resistance takes the form of mental or emotional agitation as you fight off an impending realization you don't want to have. At times resistance takes the form of sudden emotional shifts or shifts in attention, or sudden confusion. There are also times that resistance takes the form of overt self-contradiction, obvious to others, but difficult for you to recognize. Forms and patterns of resistance could easily occupy an entire book or books, so I leave it to you to make the study of your own resistance.

Keep in mind, though that most of us spend a great deal of time and energy in an ongoing effort to prevent surprises, particularly surprises that would transform us in ways over which we would have no control. Indeed, most people put tremendous effort into structuring their lives precisely to prevent such surprises. If your attitude begins to change, such that you actually want more of the truth, actually want to be transformed by it, even though you can't know in advance the nature of the transformation and wont' be able to control it, you will find truth waiting for you, always ready, always available.

Don't believe your own fibs

This might seem merely an aspect of developing and deepening your relationship with truth, and it is, but the ability to detect and ultimately reject your own internal fibs is so important that it deserves to be addressed on its own.

The most significant lies people tell themselves are usually about themselves: their nature as a person, their motivations, their supposed lack of culpability in situation after situation. Some of the behaviors involved in maintaining this system of internal lies are truly complex, but all can be placed under the simple heading of "self-deception." The self-deception falls into distinct categories, ranging from trivial and harmless to egregious and deeply harmful. Personal self-deception can also be categorized by temporal extent, anywhere from momentary and not constituting any pattern to prolonged and constituting deep and persistent patterns, even throughout the course of an entire life. Here are a couple of examples:

- Early in your life you meet someone and, in an effort to ingratiate yourself, you misrepresent your tastes in an attempt to make yourself more appealing to them. Later you feel bad about this, pledge never to repeat the dishonesty with anyone else you meet, and are able to keep your pledge. (Trivial in the initial instance, momentary, quickly corrected and without pattern.)

- As a child, you fall into a bad habit of not apologizing, which later escalates and deepens into a pattern of never being able to take responsibility for any harm you cause, which further deepens into a persistent pattern of lying to yourself about supposedly not causing any harm at all, which deepens even further into a need to blame the people you have harmed, in a now desperate effort to evade responsibility. (Egregious, lifelong, uncorrected and of a clear pattern.)

Personal self-deception also involves various motivations, again ranging from trivial to egregious. At the trivial end of the spectrum are motivations such as sparing yourself or someone else a bit of annoyance or embarrassment by telling a tiny fib, while consciously taking care to do no harm. At the truly egregious end of the spectrum are motivations such as trying to make yourself look better than you are to others by persistently lying about something, while doing serious harm to someone else through those lies, while also lying to yourself about what you are doing, and why you are doing it. Many a politician and "leader" is guilty of the latter cluster of behaviors on a daily basis.

In my experience, becoming practiced in the art of not believing your own fibs is strangely demanding. The very first barrier you encounter is the belief that you don't currently have any fibs, which is of course in itself the primary form of personal self-fibbing. Your own self-deception will nearly always masquerade as supposed virtue, or something that makes you feel better about yourself, or that seems to let you off the hook.

In the beginning of the effort to free yourself from your own self-deception, nearly all of your self-deception will be completely invisible and undetectable to you. It is only with consistent effort, the acquisition of new skill, and insistent skepticism about the stories you tell yourself that you will be able first to detect and then gradually be able to clearly identify and ultimately reject the fibs which your ego naturally generates as part of its function of trying to shield you from pain. (The ego is good at shielding you from pain in the short term, but it is precisely the cumulative effect of all of the shielding in the short term, based on self-deception, that sets you up for potentially much greater pain later on.) You should not expect to ever be completely free of your own self-deception, because fresh fibs are constantly being created by your ego. Even once you've dealt with the backlog of your self-deception of long standing, of which there may be a great deal, the best you can do from that point–if you ever even come close to reaching that point–is to become and remain truly adept at rapid detection and rejection of your own freshly minted fibs. May your personal pile of self-fibs become ever smaller. Best of luck to you!

Make the deep effort to truly understand yourself

Many people do not understand themselves well–not their own behavior, not their own motivations, not their own nature, and certainly not their own internal contradictions. A common reason we do not understand ourselves is directly related to the topic above; our attachment to our own self-deception blocks understanding, blocks recognition, blocks truth. It's not until you begin shoveling aside and discarding your personal piles of self-deception that you can make progress toward a genuine understanding of yourself. Another common reason we do not understand ourselves is that we actively want to prevent our understanding the aspects of ourselves that are unflattering, that make us feel ashamed. Of course none of us wants to experience such feelings, but without being willing to go through the dark forest, we can never reach the sunlit field.

Though sudden insight and accidental discovery can play a part, most of the work of understanding yourself is based in active self-questioning. Does your idea of yourself completely fit the evidence? Are you even interpreting the evidence correctly? Are you sure? Is there evidence you are not aware of? Is there evidence you have encountered, perhaps even repeatedly, but are excluding from consciousness, while also being unconscious of doing so? Are your stories about yourself true? Are they even the right stories? Where did you get those stories, anyway?

The good news, and I mean truly good news, is that there are times we make discoveries about ourselves that are entirely unexpected, and entirely positive. Because of my family background, for instance, it was impossible earlier in my life for me to be truly tender. I thought I was just a born hardass. Because it had been impossible for me to be tender for as long as I could remember, I was utterly amazed much later in life to discover large pools of tenderness hidden deep in my soul, from which other people could benefit, and eventually did. Perhaps there are aspects of your nature you either have never recognized, or have never had the chance to appear. Wouldn't you want to know, and sooner rather than later?

Chances are, you are not precisely what you think you are. Maybe your ideas about yourself are close to the truth, or maybe they're off by a million miles. You'll never truly know until you do the work of questioning every damn little story you tell yourself about yourself, and being willing to accept the answers that come back–the pleasant and the unpleasant, the encouraging and the discouraging, the flattering and the shameful. The benefits of this journey of discovery are too great to describe in a small book such as this. I wish you all the best on the journey of genuine self-knowledge.

Challenge yourself

Making progress in life, and making progress in your personal development require that you challenge yourself. Yet the phrase "challenge yourself" has two distinct meanings, which are directly opposed to each other. It's important to clearly distinguish between these two meanings. The more common meaning primarily involves effort and perseverance, generally does not involve deep thought, and may even require that you not think, not exercise skepticism, and not ask deep questions of yourself or others. Activities such as running a marathon, competing for salesperson of the year, or strictly adhering to an ideological doctrine represent this first meaning.

Yes, it's "challenging" to run a marathon. Running a marathon requires a tremendous effort in training over a long period of time, a vast effort of will during the training and in the event itself, and an ability to withstand stress and even periods of pain. More challenging than running a marathon, which after all is a hackneyed and conformist activity of no practical value, is to ask yourself what would be much more productive, courageous and imaginative than running a marathon, and then actually developing your own ideas, designing how to effectively execute those ideas, and then doing all the creative work as well as all the inevitable drudgery involved in brining about your own idea. Now that's truly challenging yourself, in a much deeper sense. Many people run marathons. Few people consciously develop their own ideas which transform their lives and the lives of others.

Sure, it may be a "challenge" to adhere strictly to a religious, political or spiritual doctrine. Doing so may require difficult and sustained effort, personal sacrifice, deep frustration, and disappointment with people and institutions. Yet far more challenging than adhering to a doctrine is to ask yourself difficult questions about the doctrine, questions that may fill you with fear at their implications, questions which you know–if you answer them honestly–will disrupt your systems of belief, your relationships, and possibly your livelihood and the entire structure of your life. Which is more of a challenge, adhering blindly and with great difficulty to a doctrine, or embracing the growth and transformation which are the result of questioning the doctrine? Which is more worthy?

Most people don't challenge themselves much at all, in either meaning of the term. When they do challenge themselves, it's more often in the nature of effort within predictable, conformist, well-worn patterns, than in the nature of disruptive but ultimately productive questioning and self-questioning.

Challenge Yourself: Meaning 1

Developing the ability to persevere through difficulty, cultivating willpower and toughness, learning to respond well to setbacks–all this is only of value if applied to a worthy goal. Many people admire perseverance and willpower in itself, without reference to how it is applied. That attitude is senseless and amoral. You might as well admire a CEO whose criminal activities required great perseverance. You might as well admire a serial killer for getting through the tough times in practicing his craft.

Negative examples aside, you must have these qualities of perseverance and toughness, or develop them, if you want to accomplish anything of true significance. If you don't already have the qualities of perseverance, toughness, and the ability to mange setbacks and unexpected difficulty, I would encourage you to work on developing them. All of these qualities are skills you can practice in multiple ways every day, on many different levels. As with all skills, the more you practice, and the more effectively you practice, the more you improve.

I have to practice perseverance, patience and responding well to setbacks every day, because these qualities do not come naturally to me. If my day is going well, I deliberately set myself challenges of willpower and focus in order to "stay in shape." I try to design ways to accurately measure how well I've done, so that I can assess my progress. Regularly engaging in this kind of activity on a small scale makes it easier to take on and complete projects or goals on a much larger scale, because the larger scale always consists of sets of smaller tasks. All you have to do is string together many small acts of discipline and perseverance into larger structures which gradually form major accomplishments. With practice, it becomes relatively easy to analyze a large task in terms of many small tasks, any one of which only requires a small amount of perseverance and focus. Once you become skilled at this type of analysis, even major accomplishments appear much less intimidating, because you know how to contribute toward them consistently every day.

Challenge Yourself: Meaning 2
This is the much more "challenging" meaning of "challenge yourself." If I may be blunt, have you ever wondered just how many ways you may be completely or partially full of crap? I mean no insult to you personally, of course. You've probably noticed that nearly everyone has areas of their personality, their beliefs, their attitudes, that are far from admirable, and are often quite obviously contradictory, or sloppy, or involve self-deception. It's a rare person who has the integrity and the courage to confront these aspects of their own character, and makes a project of productive self-assessment and self-improvement.

Let's take an example which is nearly universal, as well as impersonal, meaning that it is not directed at individuals. Have you ever noticed that citizens of a particular country, the United States for instance, ascribe to themselves all sorts of marvelous positive qualities, while ascribing a long list of negative qualities to people from other countries? Yet of course the people from those other countries, it will come as no surprise, are doing precisely the same thing from the opposite perspective, thinking wonderfully well of themselves, while looking down on those poor (fill in multiple negative adjectives) Americans. Now consider that nearly everyone who identifies with a group—any group, whether a racial or ethnic group, profession, age group, or ideological group—is doing exactly the same thing: patting their own backs for their own supposedly wondrous selves, while doing out harsh criticism for everyone else.

Is this not pathetic, as well as ridiculous, for everyone who does it? Is this not clearly based in a combination of ignorance, cowardice, egotism, and a lack of integrity? Does anyone who behaves with such laziness and lack of insight as well as lack of respect for honest inquiry deserve respect? You're entitled to your own opinion, but I think not.

This subject is so important, so deep and so challenging that it merits its own book, or multiple books. In the context of one short section of this small book, I will only ask you again, as politely as I can:

PART TWO: DEEPER VALUES

In what ways might you be partially or completely full of crap?

I invite you to devise your own means of answering this question, as well as your own methods of challenging yourself.

Choose useful experiences

Most people do not actively distinguish between useful experiences and useless experiences, mainly because they're too busy pursuing petty pleasures and distractions; as long as they're having fun, they don't stop to ask whether an experience is actually of value. Many people also are so oriented toward possessions that it doesn't occur to them to pay more attention to acquiring useful experiences.

There is a profound difference between spending money on material possessions, and spending money, or no money at all, on valuable experiences. An orientation toward gaining valuable experiences, the regular pursuit of valuable experiences, in itself guarantees one's further development, guarantees an increase in one's capabilities, and guarantees a deeper experience of life. Possessions offer no such guarantee, and possessions are in many cases the cause of inhibiting one's development as a person.

There is also a profound difference between paying for a useless experience and paying for a useful experience. Our economic system is supremely efficient in the production of utterly useless experiences, as well as experiences which are degrading in a literal sense: degrading of your values, degrading of your mind, degrading of your critical faculties. The choices are always arrayed before you:

1. Buying stuff that may be useless or destructive
2. Buying useless experiences that are likely also degrading
3. Buying useful experiences
4. Choosing useful experiences that cost you nothing

The best choice of all, though is a truly useful, productive experience that not only costs you nothing, but strengthens you financially and as a person. That choice is by far the best, the choice with all the advantages. The next best choice is a truly useful experience that costs nothing, is otherwise financially neutral, but enhances your life, and enhances your capacity as a person.

For the sake of clarity through contrast, let's take a closer look at the worst choices for a moment. The worst choice of all is an experience that degrades you as a person, diminishes your capacity as a person, wastes your time, wastes your money, and makes you weaker financially. You might think that people would have the sense to actively avoid such a cluster of negative aspects, yet many people actively seek out just such experiences. I know people who pay a lot of money regularly for "experiences" that provide them with nothing but reinforcement of their own stagnation, and in some cases further reinforcement of their destructive patterns. I can't call those useful experiences, and I'm not sure they even qualify as experiences, since nothing new is gained, and nothing new learned.

Given the prevalence of useless experiences, and the prevalence with which people choose useless experiences, you might conclude that it's difficult to find or create useful experiences, but quite the opposite is true. Opportunities for useful experience are everywhere, at every moment. All you have to do is recognize them, choose them, and get in the habit of choosing them.

Furthermore, it isn't difficult at all to determine what would be a useful experience. All you have to do is ask yourself: What would add to me as a person? Just consider that one question, evaluate the ideas that arise in your mind, and select a particularly good one. Of course the precise nature of the choice will be different for each person, but the process is simple. For some people it might be doing something they're nervous about trying but they know would be good for them. For others it might be taking a class, or meeting new people, or something as large as a shift in career. For others it might be more internal, like giving up a bad habit of dwelling on painful memories. The point is to deliberately choose an experience that adds new understanding, new insight, or new capabilities to you as a person.

Keep in mind that a useful experience may be fun, not fun at all, or anywhere in between. Whether the experience itself is pleasurable or not is completely irrelevant as to whether it is useful. Obviously, if you can find or create experiences that are both useful and fun, you should give preference to those experiences, but don't ever confuse fun with useful. They're not at all the same thing, and many a fun experience is utterly useless, and many an unpleasant experience is truly useful.

Exercise: Design or choose a useful experience
Speaking of fun, this is a fun exercise, one that should become a constant part of your life. If you do this exercise regularly, you'll never go stale, and never be bored. The exercise is also infinitely variable, because there is always more to learn, and there are always new ways to grow. The exercise itself is simple, though there are many different

PART TWO: DEEPER VALUES

areas to which you can apply it. Here are a few, to give you some ideas:

- *expand your awareness*
- *develop a new skill*
- *increase your emotional capability*
- *improve an area of your behavior, or even your personality*
- *enter an environment rich in opportunity*
- *choose an experience the effect of which you can't predict*

You should be able to think of additional areas yourself, and I encourage you to do so.

Some approaches to the exercise are much more challenging than others. It's easy to sign up for a packaged experience, such as a dance class, a tour, a book club, or a professional development program. It's much more difficult to think deeply about who you are, where you came from, what's wonderful about you but also how you're broken, and most of all how you can design an entire set of experiences from scratch to build new aspects of yourself. By far the most challenging approach is to ask yourself with complete bluntness "What truly sucks about me, and how could I fix it?" and then insist on an honest answer.

Most people will gravitate toward the middle of this spectrum. Of course you should do what feels right for you, but please don't just be a wimp. Don't fool yourself into thinking you're choosing a useful experience if you don't really learn a damn thing of any importance from it, and above all don't just keep choosing the same thing or the same category again and again, because that would mean you had turned an exercise meant to promote growth into a mechanism for guaranteed stagnation. If you're not sure what I mean by that, here's an example: Someone who is obsessed with cooking and uses cooking as a way of avoiding new experiences and keeping life at bay isn't exactly being brave or taking on something new by learning more about French sauces. Likewise someone who loves sports isn't exactly expanding their horizons by taking up yet another sport. The crucial point is to try entirely new areas periodically, areas about which you know little or nothing, areas that may make you a bit nervous, areas in which you know you'll be surprised, and learn deeply. Gradually gain broad experience with this exercise, so that you can apply it again and again in your life, and continue to add new areas of understanding and capability.

I use this exercise frequently, and at multiple levels. On the highest level, I make sure that I am taking on major new experiences in different areas over the course of years, and specifically in order to add new areas of awareness, and to work on both improving certain areas of my personality, and adding new aspects to my personality. I also use the exercise on a microscopic, moment-to-moment level at many points during every day, challenging myself in the moment to depart from comfortable, fixed patterns of thought, emotional response and behavior, and then observe and learn from the results. I use specific forms of the exercise in piano practice and in art projects in order to generate new inspiration and new discoveries, but also use the exercise very broadly, making sure that I occasionally embark on categories of experience that are unfamiliar to me, but that I know will be useful.

Exercise: Take an inventory of yourself regarding useful experiences
Developing the habit of regularly seeking out useful experiences is so important that it's good to periodically take stock of yourself in this regard. Ask yourself the following questions:

- *When was the last time I had a truly useful experience, one that added to my understanding, insight, and abilities?*
- *What has been the proportion of useful experience versus useless experience in my life recently?*
- *Have I set aside time and energy in my life for further truly useful experiences?*
- *Am I giving preference for "packaged" experiences, such as tours or classes, rather than choosing and creating my own?*

- *Am I avoiding certain categories of experience, even though I know how important they are, because I feel nervous or insecure?*
- *How can I incorporate into my life a higher proportion of useful experiences?*

Expand your mind

Deliberately and persistently making efforts to expand your own mind is one of the most productive choices you can make in your entire life. Few people do this, unfortunately. Most do the opposite, clinging tightly to familiar patterns and comfortable, if stultifying repetition of behavior on all levels–mental, emotional, social. This one choice of whether to grow or whether to cling can determine whether you live an interesting life, and become a grownup in the most deeply positive sense of the term, or you lead a boring life, and never truly grow up.

Clearly, expanding your mind can be the result of choosing new stimulating external experiences, as described in the section above, but you can also expand your mind without any external stimulus at all. This might sound a bit strange to those not familiar with the process, but purely through opening yourself up to new perceptions, or engaging with deep questions, or deliberately redirecting your attention in ways that generate new insight, you can radically expand your mind through a purely internal process. The truth is that at any point you could, without any external experience or external stimulation, fundamentally expand your mind. This is only a matter of making the choice, putting in the effort, and being willing to be transformed by the process.

I am in favor of both methods, because the two methods have different advantages, differ in their nature and their results, and differ in their implications. Most people not only never make an effort to expand their mind, but put a lot of effort into warding off influences that might expand their mind, though they are in most cases unconsciously selective in what they avoid or deflect or reject. For those unusual people who actively seek to expand their mind, some rely strongly on the external method, and have not developed much ability to do so through an internal process. Others are able to expand their mind through an internal process, and do not rely so much on external experiences. Most people who are motivated toward expanding their mind use both methods, though usually strongly favor one method or the other, if only as a matter of habit. Yet everyone who is motivated to expand their mind can benefit from becoming fully adept in both approaches.

By this point, when I meet someone, I can very quickly identify whether they are drawn to mind expansion, or averse to it. Within my own mind, I label this MindExpansion-philic or MindExpansion-phobic. In the case of people I meet who are ME-philic, I can also very quickly tell which method they favor, external or internal. I'm not certain how I am able to sense this, but it is absolutely obvious to me within a few minutes of interacting with someone.

Once again, this topic could easily occupy another entire book or books, so for the moment I leave it to you as to areas in which you expand your mind, and the methods you use to do so.

Develop your curiosity

Curiosity is a vast advantage that can carry you very far in life. Without deep curiosity, it is not possible to advance very far in knowledge or ability. Without deep curiosity, it is not possible to develop very far as a human being. Without deep curiosity, stasis will inevitably set in, preventing you from reaching the higher levels of awareness which can transform you and your life for the better. Many a deep and damaging rut is the result of insufficient curiosity.

Some people naturally have a lot of curiosity, others have less, and some either have little to none, or have suppressed their curiosity out of fear. Yet the kind of deep curiosity which can produce powerful realizations and expanded awareness is not a personal, unchangeable quality, not a fixed character trait at all. It is mostly a habit, and for the people who have strong and consistent curiosity, the habit of pursuing and achieving understanding of what was of interest to them took hold long ago, and is now a fundamental aspect of their being.

Curiosity can also be a commitment however, even for those who do not have the habit of curiosity, and even for those who are afraid of where curiosity might lead them. Once you begin to understand how much deep curiosity can do for you, and also begin to understand how much a lack of curiosity can limit you and limit the possibilities for you and for your life, a commitment to curiosity becomes a matter of making the choice to take advantage of all that curiosity can provide for you.

Merely accepting a clear advantage doesn't sound like a commitment at all though, just a selfish choice. If curiosity can provide so much benefit, why wouldn't everyone be infinitely curious at all times, and in all situations? Clearly that is not at all the case. The answer lies in the price to be paid for a true commitment, whether to a marriage, a career, a significant accomplishment, or a moral position at odds with your society. If a commitment only involves the easy and the pleasant, it's either not much of a commitment, or a commitment which has not been tested. The essence of true commitment is the willingness to pay a price for that commitment, and submit to the implications of that commitment.

The commitment to curiosity can be a rough road indeed: steep, winding, bumpy, dark, gusty, at times frightening, and certainly full of surprises, not all of them pleasant. But the payoff of the journey is extraordinary. That payoff is a combination of knowledge, deep understanding, advanced mental and emotional capability, flexibility, practice in persistence and productively managing discomfort, but most of all the advantage is fearlessness–the kind of fearlessness that creates wonderful new possibilities, and actually makes it easier to pursue major accomplishments.

How does this fearlessness come about, through curiosity? The easiest way to describe this is to first make the point that fear is the opposite of curiosity. Fear kills curiosity, and can kill it quickly. When someone is afraid of where understanding might lead, even if mistaken in that fear, the last thing they want is to become curious about a genuine answer. They fear the answer, so curiosity is their enemy, and they kill that enemy within them. Yet because curiosity is the opposite of fear, curiosity has its own power, and can conquer fear. Practicing curiosity thus is practicing fearlessness. With consistent, strong practice over time, you can become *very* good at this. Choose curiosity. Choose to practice curiosity, as much as you can stand, every day. In the process, you'll learn a tremendous amount, and develop the habit of fearlessness, both of which can carry you further than you can imagine–which leads directly to the next topic.

Develop your imagination
Effective imagination is a crucial asset, without which major forms of progress are impossible. Imagination is actually the engine of most progress, because it embodies deep wishes, powerful emotions, and the ability to navigate effectively toward a goal. Many people are held back in their personal progress specifically because they don't or can't "picture themselves" doing something, or becoming something, even when the benefits of taking action toward that vision are clear, even

when not taking action toward that vision is costly, and even painful. Many people spend much of their lives in misery specifically because they don't or can't imagine their way out of their current conditions, or habits, or attachments, or identity.

Yet imagination is not at all an ability you either have or don't have. Imagination is a skill, or rather a set of skills. Those skills can be learned, practiced, continually improved and continually expanded. You can become *very good* at using your imagination to bring about positive changes in your life, but there's a catch. The catch is that there are two types of imagination, and unless you use both of them, true progress may still not be possible. That there are two distinct types of imagination is conveyed by the ambivalence accorded imagination, which is given either a positive or a negative value, depending on the circumstances and the type of imagination.

The first type of imagination, often assigned a negative value, is fantasy. Children are exhorted to "stop daydreaming." A "dreamer" is someone who can't seem to actually get anything done. It is "the stuff of fantasy" that is derided as useless, a waste of time. Yet it is precisely this first type of imagination, that of fantasizing which, if coupled with the second type, can produce astounding results.

This second type of imagination I will call practical imagination, which means imagining in precise terms how to accomplish something. Practical imagination is in a sense the opposite of fantasy; while fantasy is detached from current reality, practical imagination is based in reality, and depends on accurate judgment based in reality. There are people whose fantasy life may be close to non-existent but who, if you give them an unusual task to accomplish, can quickly imagine all the steps that would be necessary, even if those steps involve something that has never been done before. They'll also be right about almost everything involved, because they will have thought it all through in purely practical terms in their imagination. That's practical imagination at work. People with a highly developed practical imagination may have little ability in fantasy, but fantasy is just as important and just as valuable as practical imagination, though in an entirely different way.

Fantasy is valuable specifically because it frees us from the strictures and confines of current reality, and provides a vision of a possibly better reality. Fantasy allows us to venture beyond anything we have ever experienced in reality, and then bring what we experienced in fantasy back with us into the "real" world, such as it is.

PART TWO: DEEPER VALUES

The truly important task is the linking together of the two types of imagination: translating fantasy into practical steps which will transform the fantasy into reality. There's little point in "daydreaming," unless you're going to do the work of turning a compelling daydream into a set of actions that will translate the daydream into reality, and allow you to actually live it.

This is where the tension between the two types of imagination comes into play. Without far-ranging fantasy, you're not getting far enough away from the deficiencies of current reality to make much of a difference. If you reign in and inhibit your fantasy too much by dismissing in advance its apparent impracticality, you're just hobbling your ability to imagine anything much better than what exists already. Yet if your fantasy is too detached from reality, it has no chance of ever being transformed into reality, and is then properly labeled "pointless daydreaming." The best of both worlds is to give full free reign to your fantasy so that you aren't restricting the range of your imagination unnecessarily in advance, while also developing your judgment as to which fantasies can or could be transformed into reality, and becoming adept at pursuing with practical imagination the fantasies rich with genuine possibility.

I don't know how many times I've written these words already in this small book, but this subject also merits an entire book of its own. Developing your skill in both effective fantasy and practical imagination as well as the skill of linking the two together to transform your dreams into reality consists only of precisely that: a set of skills you can identify, practice and develop further. Developing these combined skills can ope the route to a truly amazing life. I wish you the best of success in doing so.

Work to become more creative

Why is creativity important? Partly because without creativity, you are stuck with what comes your way–and what comes your way may indeed suck–but mostly because creativity provides you ways to generate new and better possibilities in your life. Creativity and fantasy overlap, but creativity involves more than the ability to fantasize, though the ability to fantasize is inherent in creativity. Creativity, though it may seem mysterious or even magical, is just another set of skills which can be practiced, developed, expanded and deepened.

The essence of creativity is the ability to say "yes," even to what at first may appear ridiculous, or impractical, or perhaps a terrible or even offensive idea. The essence of creativity is to "go with it," and then see where "it" takes you, and benefit and learn from doing so. Thus, the fundamental skill of creativity is an emotional skill and a social skill, or rather an anti-social skill: the emotional ability to ignore the "no" that human beings pronounce so readily, to ignore the "no" that people will say to you directly, and to ignore the "no" that even appears in your own mind, because you've been trained to say it so much yourself. Whether you think of creativity as saying "yes" or as "gagging the censor," as the pathway to new and greater possibilities, or just as a way to have fun, creativity in some form should always be part of your life. You should always be making an effort to become better at being creative, in whatever ways and in whatever areas you choose.

If you are one of those people who think they aren't very creative, your first creative act should be to imagine yourself as more creative, and then use your practical imagination to gradually make yourself so. What could be a more creative project than to make yourself more creative, and then benefit from your own increased creativity?

Develop and refine your judgment

"By three methods we may learn wisdom: First, by reflection, which is noblest; Second, by imitation, which is easiest; and third by experience, which is the bitterest."

— Confucius (551 B.C.E.-479 B.C.E.)

Your greatest asset is the quality of your judgment. Consider, at an extreme, where bad judgment can lead: destructive relationships, bad health, debt, prison, death. Yes, the quality of your judgment really is as serious as that. No one is born with excellent judgment. It has to be developed, maintained, and refined over time.

One of the best ways to do this is to keep a set of notes about judgments you make: of people, situations, attitudes, activities, what you consider valuable or not valuable. Occasionally review your judgments and try to find flaws in those judgments, with the goal of improving your judgment, either in general or in specific areas you've identified as weak or problematic.

If you ever discover you were wrong in a judgment you made, you have a marvelous opportunity to discover exactly how and why your judgment was flawed. Perhaps you were lazy, or prejudiced. Perhaps you overlooked something because your perception is weak in that area. Perhaps mistaken loyalty or your own ego unduly influenced you. Whatever may be the cause of your flawed judgment, be honest with yourself. The goal is to improve your judgment, not pretend you're perfect. Take pride in admitting to yourself that you made a mistake, and plan to improve yourself so that you don't make the same or similar mistakes in the future.

Carefully choose noble commitments

Each word in the short title of this section is ripe with meaning, and was chosen deliberately, in order to distinguish between commitments that are chosen carefully, or chosen carelessly; truly chosen or not truly chosen; noble or not noble. Let's review these aspects, one by one.

Many commitments are not truly chosen consciously. The most severe example of unchosen commitments exists in the form of all the children born only because their parents wanted to have sex. Did those parents choose the commitment of a lifetime to an innocent young human being? No, not at all. They just wanted the sex, at the time they wanted it. This example is particularly glaring as well as particularly prevalent, but there are many others in other areas of life: profession, relationships, social affiliations, political affiliations. People just drift into commitments that are not consciously chosen.

Many commitments are chosen, but not chosen carefully. Often people fall into a commitment, without giving the precise nature of the commitment or the implications of the commitment much thought. Most of us have had the experience of pledging a commitment, only later to realize that we should have given far more thought to what the commitment meant, and what the commitment would involve. Ever backed out of a commitment without much grace? That was probably a commitment you didn't think about carefully enough in advance.

It might sound strange, but people also make commitments which are not only less than noble, but in some cases far from noble, and at times unethical or even criminal. Such unfortunate commitments are often the result of ties of obligation, or perceived obligation, or of social or professional affiliation. For instance, a gang member may make a "commitment" to a despicable, immoral act of violence, a commitment that stems directly from affiliation with the gang. Many such negative commitments also exist in the corporate world, the world of government, the military, international relations, and even the family. How many acts of sexual abuse have been covered up by a "commitment" not to tell, a "commitment" to a relationship with the abuser? Religion, supposedly a region of higher morality, also often results in immoral commitments.

Clearly, it's better to consciously and carefully choose commitments, but what would be examples of a "noble commitment?" We tend to think of a "noble commitment" as publicly visible, a matter of potential admiration from others, yet a noble commitment can be in any area, and of any extent, and many of the choices as to noble commitment may not seem of the nature of "commitment" as commonly construed. We tend to think of commitments as directed to a cause, or a relationship, or a proposed accomplishment, but a deep commitment to a noble ideal is often more valuable, and of greater true significance. For instance, you may choose to make a deep commitment to genuinely understand other people, instead of taking the easy path of judging them. That is indeed a noble commitment, requiring effort, patience, perseverance and fortitude. Yet that commitment is only visible to others in a subtle way, only over time, and no one is going to publicly present you with an award for that commitment. You may choose to make a deep commitment to self-improvement, one of the most noble commitments any person can make, yet you need not tell anyone, and it's better to let the results speak for themselves.

I don't mean to in any way denigrate commitments to specific other people, or particular organizations or accomplishments, but in my experience it is commitments which have at their core a universal value which are most important, most far-reaching, and ultimately of greatest significance.

I encourage you to make your own carefully chosen noble commitments. The results are always far better than those of bad commitments, or sloppy commitments, or commitments you didn't even realize you were making.

Learn to love the small, modest, free and unencumbered

Many people have trouble with the idea that you can fundamentally change what you want, what you appreciate, what you are attracted to. They seem to feel that their current preferences represent their absolute identity, and that the idea of deliberately altering their own preferences

PART TWO: DEEPER VALUES

constitutes a threat to their identity. That response makes no sense. This is why:

You adopted many of your preferences earlier in your life unconsciously, and then simply got used to them, and began to think of them as representing your identity. Had you been raised in different circumstances—social, psychological material, cultural—you would have unconsciously adopted a very different set of preferences, and thus a different identity. Therefore your preferences are fundamentally random and not based, in most cases, on values. To base your identity on preferences which were formed unconsciously is not at all a strong form of identity.

By this time in your life you are, presumably, far more conscious. You are now in a position to examine and reflect on questions of values, ethics, morality, what you consider good and productive and helpful, and exactly why. To continue to base your identity on preferences, many of which were formed before you were able to consciously evaluate them, would mean continuing an identity which has a weak basis, and is probably full of inconsistencies and contradictions.

Wouldn't it be better to now consciously examine your own values, and then consciously choose preferences based on those consciously considered and chosen values? Wouldn't your preferences and habits then be more consistent and less contradictory? Wouldn't your very identity, in fact, be more harmonious?

This process of consciously examining and critiquing your own values is a highly personal one, and a deep subject in itself. I leave the details of that process entirely to you. I assure you from my own experience that the process itself is tremendously fulfilling, if also deeply challenging. The end result, however is great clarity of motivation, and much more effective, consistent and coordinated action; you know exactly what you are doing, and most important of all you know exactly why.

This has all been a necessary introduction to the issue raised at the beginning of this section of deliberately changing your own preferences. When you decide to change your own preferences based on values, the process is both exhilarating and fascinating. It can feel almost like designing a new self, because preferences and identity are so strongly intertwined. Yet when you know that you are only adjusting your preferences based on deeper values which represent deeper aspects of your identity, it's more a matter of asserting your deeper identity by bringing more aspects of your behavior into alignment with that deeper identity.

So here you are, embedded within consumerist society, bombarded by advertising which attempts to inject into you specific desires for specific mostly idiotic products, all for the sake of someone else's profit, in nearly all cases the profit of someone unknown to you, whose values are probably questionable, and quite possibly repugnant. The consumerist society which surrounds you is doing everything it can to convince you that you need to buy all the junk it's pushing at you, and will swiftly label you a loser if you don't conform. What's one clear alternative to all this?

Learn to love the small, modest, free and unencumbered.

You can gradually shift your attention, your appreciation and your desires toward things that cost you nothing, are beautifully modest, readily available, and aren't going to tempt you to do anything truly idiotic like get your entire kitchen remodeled at great expense just because your neighbor got theirs remodeled because their neighbor got theirs remodeled.

What might these small, modest, free and unencumbered things be? The most obvious examples come from nature, but there are many other possibilities, and once you begin to shift your attention to such things, you will eventually discover an unlimited abundance of possibilities. What is required, though is that you open your mind completely to new ways to appreciate the physical world, and that you give up all concern with whether what you come to appreciate is assigned any value at all by the society in which you live. One of the truly wonderful aspects of learning this new kind of appreciation and shift in what you desire is that if you share this experience with others, you will find other people with whom you can form deep bonds of meaning that go far beyond your individual egos. You will probably also find that a lot of people think you've gone a bit nuts. That's ok, because their response is useful information about them, and they literally do not know what they are missing.

Exercise: Find something small, modest, free and unencumbered
If you are someone who tends to relate very strongly and exclusively to the things that are valued socially by others, this exercise may be particularly challenging for you. This is a very important exercise however, so if you don't succeed the first time, make some adjustments in your approach, and try again until the magic begins to work for you. This is also an exercise to use again and again as needed, especially if you feel yourself falling back into conformity to the pressure to relate to what other people care about, or what other people are paying attention to, or what other people are buying.

First, relax into a state in which you can turn your attention freely to small physical details. It's good to pick up some small object you already appreciate and enjoy, examine its smaller details, and try to notice new details. Then head out to an area in which you're likely to encounter interesting objects. The choice as to exactly what type of environment or what type of objects is completely up to you. For some people it will be a hiking trail, or a beach, or a stony riverbed. For others it may be a quirky urban environment, an abandoned lot, or the ruins of a factory. You could also just walk along a route that is already familiar to you, but with the goal of being completely receptive to noticing new aspects. Take your time. Sink into the experience of noticing the smallest details. If you can take a magnifying glass along, all the better.

When you find something you like a lot, as long as you wouldn't be stealing and are confident no one would miss what has captured your attention, take it home with you, and put it out on display. I have no idea what will appeal to you, but I have fallen in love with small stones, pieces of wood, leaves, pine cones, shells, some pieces of copper wire discarded in a dumpster, a small entryway rug with a beautifully simple design I found tossed on the street, a large but very flexible industrial spring, and a large battered sheet of thick aluminum I found in the Feather River in California. I turned the sheet of aluminum into a unique coffee table by putting it on top of the large spring. I had created a coffee table that wiggled, for many seconds, once set in motion. It was a coffee table that stirred my coffee, by wiggling. I absolutely loved it.

If you find the right objects for you, your taste, and your personality, you may be amazed what pleasure they bring you over the years, including the pleasure both of knowing that you didn't have to pay for them, and the memory of the unique experience of finding them.

"A better definition of wealth is how many valuable experiences you have had."

– Anonymous

Expand your identity

Identity is a strange matter, in many ways. To say that most people are terribly attached to their own identity is to state the obvious. Yet most people also, even while clinging to their own identity (or rather what they think of as their identity), wish other people would change in significant ways, in effect changing their identity. There is perhaps no more fundamental double standard than insisting that others alter their identity while you cling to yours. Most people also, giving the matter any true thought, realize that everyone's identity is largely a matter of random circumstances, and that given the randomness of the origins of identity, it makes little sense to be so attached to something so random. In addition, our identity has actually changed in fundamental ways throughout our lives, and yet we persist with a sense of identity despite all these changes. In a way, identity is like a complex map with a moving dot on it, and no matter where you are in the complex terrain, it always says "You are here."

Given the actual fluidity of identity despite the common emotional attachment to a false idea of fixed identity, the ability to consciously expand your identity provides a tremendous advantage. First of all, you become free of the hypocrisy of wanting others to change, while you cling to your identity. Your identity becomes a matter of conscious fluidity, conscious expansion, and your "identity" becomes more a matter of commitment to expansion of identity than to any particular limited form of identity. A bit of personal explanation is in order.

Early in my life I experienced deep, vidid insights about many of the people I encountered. The most productive insight, but also the most frustrating in certain ways, had to do with the way most people define and experience their identity according to fixed, rigid social categories. I realized, or rather I witnessed directly as a matter of insight, that the categories operating in people's minds had no genuine basis, but were merely socially imposed concepts which formed a kind of prison of identity of which the person was generally not aware, making the prison all the more effective. Not only that, but these confining categories were made even more rigid and more confining through their adhesion within the mind to specific words which represented the category. All this struck me as both hideous and ridiculous at the same time. I wanted no part of it.

Naturally, I began experimenting within my own mind and my own social environment with the nature of these categories, and how to recognize their existence and operation in others, and how to become adept at dealing with them as they existed in others, while abandoning them within myself. What sorts of categories am I referring to? Sex, gender, ethnicity, intelligence, accomplishment, level of education, social status, authority, nationality: all these and more I understood as social illusions forming a matrix of psychological and social imprisonment from which one could free oneself not through an act of will or resistance, but through relaxation, imagination, and active, loving appreciation of the infinite aspects of raw physical reality.

If it's difficult for you to imagine functioning without these socially imposed structures, consider the obvious fact that most animals are able to live their entire lives without most of the categories human beings cling to so tenaciously, and yet animals function with tremendous subtlety in their behavior, are able to adapt and learn, and are in many ways more aware than we are.

Your identity is not fixed. After all, your identity has been changing throughout your life, and continues to change. Yet at each point along the way, you live within an illusion that your identity is stable. Once you accept that your identity is not fixed, but is always changing and therefore always changeable, you begin to wonder how much of your identity can be consciously chosen, instead of being the unconscious result of background and experience and hardened habit. Can you make a project of consciously altering your own identity? Of course you can, because identity, after all is mainly a matter of how you think about yourself.

An example from my own life is that I used to think of myself as an American. As I learned more about actual American history, not the syrupy myths passed off as American history, I found this identification not only confining, but in many ways negative. Gradually I shifted my identity consciously toward moral values and toward ideals of justice, personal development, mercy and understanding, and away from nationality. I no longer identify with any nationality at all. I recognize the category of nationality within others, and recognize the operation of that category within others, yet I choose not to relate to the category within myself.

In a similar way, I long ago abandoned any gender identity. I found all gender identity terribly confining, and ultimately ridiculous. Once again, I recognize in detail the workings of gender identity in others, but I abstain from that aspect of identity myself. Instead, I identify with the deeper values of the effort toward greater awareness, striving toward the good and the productive in all things, with creativity, shared consciousness with others, and conscious collaboration toward positive goals.

What we normally think of as identity is only a set of conceptual frames. Different frames produce different results, and some frames are far better than others. Not to pick on gender, though I certainly love to do so, but there are many biological males whose major behavioral problems stem mostly from their identification as male, instead of an identification that produces a more interesting, more creative, more positive result. Such people are hung up on thinking of themselves as male, instead of thinking of themselves as kind, or caring, or full of deep curiosity, or in love with learning, or eager to embrace and absorb truth, and be transformed through surrender to the process. They think they're guys, so they are and remain so, though they could at any moment become something much better, through a fundamental shift in identification.

The number and variety of possible frames through which you can construct your identity is infinite. Most people operate based on a small set of frames which are mostly either unconscious, or not critically evaluated. Yet at any point, you can consciously choose other frames, other ways of thinking about yourself and, after critically evaluating them, add them to your repertoire.

PART TWO: DEEPER VALUES

Some examples are easier for most people to deal with than others. For instance, it's not much of a challenge for someone from one country to imagine identifying with a nationality they perceive as roughly similar to their own, or not too distant: Americans and Canadians, or Germans and Austrians, for example. Yet did you realize that you also always have a choice, on a fundamental level, as to whether you identify as a human being? Yes, the choice is yours, and there are good reasons to choose not to restrict your identity to that of a mere human being. After all, you are a spirit in human form, not just a human being with a spirit. There are major advantages to transcending identification as a human being–but that's the subject of another entire book, yet to be written.

I encourage you to experiment. Ask yourself what the likely effect would be of thinking of yourself in a particular new way, and use your imagination in this process. This process can be extraordinarily fun and enlivening. You can even deliberately choose to think of yourself as all kinds of things you actually are not at all, in a purely physical sense, and have great fun with this process.

Exercise: Just who do you think you think you are, or aren't?
Set aside at least twenty minutes for this exercise, and possibly more. Take as much time as you want, and come back to this exercise as many times and in as many ways as you feel is helpful to you. This may be the most fundamentally important exercise in the book. This one exercise offers a way to create new opportunities for you on multiple levels. First we must establish the context. The actual exercise follows the short essay below.

You have an identity, a self-concept. Unfortunately that self-concept, which you think of as your own, was determined mostly by your society. It's not actually yours at all. The primary reason for this is that the categories you use to think about yourself were defined by your society, not by you. Unless you've done the very difficult, detailed work of designing your own categories and applying them consistently, and choosing which ones to use under what conditions, you exist in a maze of categories not of your own creation, not of your own design, not of your own choosing, and have no way of thinking of yourself except through categories that were created and enforced by the impersonal forces of society.

In addition, this confining mesh of categories which operates in and on your mind is rigidly attached to the primary means you use to communicate: words. Perhaps you're not convinced, so I will demonstrate. Clear your mind, and prepare yourself to observe your own reactions emotionally, socially and in terms of judgment to the following list of words and phrases:

    A-type personality
    bitch
    control freak
    exhibitionist
    loser
    user
    prick
    princess
    introvert
    show-off
    brown-noser
    mama's boy
    piece of shit
    party girl
    odd-man-out
    loner
    cry baby
    man about town
    heart breaker
    lady killer
    narcissist
    snot-nosed kid
    creep
    just another pretty face

Had enough? I hope you noticed that every one of those words or short phrases not only has a powerful emotional impact, but also brings with it a complex set of associations, a strong social judgment, and perhaps even a payload of personal memories of people you thought of according to some of the labels listed, or people who made it clear they thought of you according to some of the labels listed.

Think of the number of times–the total number of times in your entire life–that you made use of any of these labels either as a listener, a speaker, or just within your own mind. The number is certainly in the thousands, and the list above is nowhere near complete. This means that if we had a more complete list, you would have made use of these categories and the words representing the categories, tens of thousands of times, and perhaps hundreds of thousands of times in

PART TWO: DEEPER VALUES

your life so far. That's an awful lot of times to be using something you've probably never questioned, and didn't consciously choose.

So what are these categories, exactly? Where did they come from? Who invented them, exactly how were they defined, and who chose the word or phrase to represent them? All of them are the result of social judgments by groups, and they were formed over time through an anonymous and impersonal social process. There is no one you can call up on the phone or meet with to to try to renegotiate the structure and precise meaning of those concepts. Yet you are constantly making use of them within yourself, judging yourself with reference to these labels, and every one of those labels and the social judgments they convey are a means of enforcement, a means of punishment, a means of control.

We've gone far enough for the moment. You get the idea. This subject is so vast that to deal with it completely would require another entire book, or several books. Let's jump right into the exercise.

How would you describe yourself? I mean how would you, the deepest inner you, the you that exists on a level entirely apart from society, how would that "you" describe yourself, without using or even referring to any of the categories or labels society uses to control you? Use words for this, but the words you use will be your own, and the categories you refer to will be your own, of your own design and your own choosing, with labels for the categories that you invented yourself. If you notice clichés or standard labels creeping in, you're getting off track, so bring yourself back to your self.

The point of this exercise is to gain practice in choosing ways of thinking about yourself and other people which are more flexible, more free, more fair, more detailed, more subtle, and most of all preserve and expand the possibilities for all of us.

Here are a few examples of exactly the approach not to take:

"I am a middle-aged, highly educated black female who works hard, but keeps her sexy side."

"I am a piece of shit. I've always been a loser, and I'm just not good at anything. I should probably do everyone a favor and just kill myself."

"I'm really very successful. I may not have everything, but at least I like myself, and other people like me, too. You could call me a straight-up kind of guy."

Here's an example you may or may not identify with, but certainly is free of the usual confining categories:

"I am a consciousness, a gaze that embraces. I am a blending and bending of light, a becoming of what I observe, a force that is its own force, transformed by and transforming other forces. I am nothing, and yet myself. I am a smile that learns, and hangs in the air, waiting for another smile to learn with, smile with, and be with."

See the difference? The first three self-descriptions were based entirely on categories created by society through an impersonal process. They are rigid, and confining. The fourth self-description is entirely different, not at all based on categories generated by society. The fourth self-description is also tremendously expansive and, unlike the first three self-descriptions, suggests much greater possibilities.

Write a description of yourself that is as free from the crude, confining categories dictated by society as you can. It may take a few iterations of the exercise to navigate away from the common categories, and discover a new way of describing yourself as a spirit. If you sink deeply into this exercise, you may discover a whole new world within yourself.

Expand your identity specifically through travel

The experience of freedom during travel is due only in part to exposure to new environments. Much of this experience is also due to being free of your stuff, your stuff that confines you to particular behaviors and attitudes, particular relationships, and particular obligations, but most of all to a particular identity, a particular limited idea of yourself.

I know many people who travel extensively, but I've also noticed certain serious differences in approaches to travel as an experience. Some people learn deeply from their travel experiences, and become greater human beings in the process. They are able to absorb new, surprising experiences, and incorporate those experiences into an expanded awareness, an appreciation of the diversity of cultures and ways of life, and conditions of life. They view travel as a way to expand their own identity, through greater understanding.

Then there are the people who travel, and may travel to exactly the same places as the first type of person, but they return without having changed in any way, without having been truly affected in any way, without having learned anything important. They just saw a bunch of sights, or possibly didn't even really see anything, though they may have flown across the world to an entirely new environment, and an entirely different culture. It's as though they have a mental and emotional shield up all the time which prevents them from absorbing new experience.

The first group tends to travel light; they don't bring much of their own stuff with them. The second group tends to travel with as much of their own stuff from "back home" as possible. That's part of their problem; they travel with a heavy, complex load of reminders of their identity—or what they think is their identity—to which they cling, no matter where they are. The more exotic the environs, the more of their own stuff they bring, and the tighter they cling to it. They should probably just stay home, since they clearly intend not to actually experience anything new.

Then there are the people who travel in order to take as many pictures as possible, usually of exactly the same things all the other tourists take pictures of, often pictures of exactly the things they've already seen many pictures of on the web, in documentaries, and in travel brochures. Whenever they take a picture, it's as though they're just checking something off a list, and all they have in mind while they're "away" is everyone back home they can send the pictures to. Their body has traveled, but their mind and spirit are still back home. They see only through the camera, even in their own mind, and then only through a small set of preconceived notions of what pictures they can share with the people they already know. For many of these people, it never even occurs to them to meet anyone in the place to which they've traveled. They might as well have just stayed home and copied a bunch of sightseeing pictures off the web and sent them to their friends, as though they had actually gone somewhere, because either way, they didn't actually go anywhere.

There is a deep, defining difference between going to Moscow on a tour and seeing the Kremlin, Red Square, St. Basil's Cathedral, and the Tretyakov Museum, on the one hand, versus going to Moscow and meeting some gypsies by the side of the road who are completely impressed by your lack of fear and therefore take a liking to you and share some absurd humor with you, then embarking on a random walk in the rain and deliberately getting lost but having an amazing conversation, mainly through gesture, with a kindly old man in a tattered overcoat to whom you give a few rubles when he excitedly gives you directions to somewhere you don't even want to go, then getting on the subway and riding randomly all over the city deep underground, while walking up and down the subway cars to look closely at all the people, and the books they are reading, and their strangely precious clothes, and their manner indefinably different in infinite ways from yours, then going to Red Square and eating a couple of pieces of pizza at the Sbarro near the McDonald's with its sign in Cyrillic (**Макдоналдс**) while sitting next to a six-foot-tall poorly spray-painted styrofoam copy of the Statue of Liberty. I'll take the second set of experiences, thank you.

I advocate travel as a means of radical learning, of radical expansion of your identity. Don't get on that cruise ship. Don't sign up for that tour. Don't go with your friends. Head out to new lands with a mind on fire with curiosity, a heart fully open to people very different from you, and completely free from your usual frames of reference. You'll have a much deeper, much more significant experience, but you'll only be able to describe it to people who want to know. That way you'll also find out who actually wants to know and understand, instead of just look at the usual terribly predictable set of travel pictures.

Speaking of travel pictures, be very careful with your camera. That camera of yours can easily become a primary means of blocking new experience, of preventing genuinely new experience from penetrating your identity. It's all too easy to become involved in "capturing" moments, with the implicit thought of how they will look from your existing frames of reference, which only serves to remind you and to tie you again and again to your previous frames of references. The camera can all too easily become a psychological barrier between you and all the richness you could experience directly, and add to your identity. There is also of course the matter of ruining your experience of travel by staying in touch by email with your pre-existing frames of reference. If you're still connected all the time to your home base, did you actually go anywhere, socially, emotionally, mentally, psychologically?

Sink deeply into the purely local experiences, as they happen. Don't "frame" them, either with a camera, or by electronic tether, or even within your own mind. Travel truly. Truly travel.

Imagine yourself as a different person

Each of us limited in so many ways. We are limited by our background, by our personality, by how we think of ourselves, by our social affiliations, by our habits of mind and emotion. Those

PART TWO: DEEPER VALUES

limitations prevent some of the most wonderful and productive possibilities from entering our lives. One of the most effective ways to break free of your current limitations is to vividly and deeply imagine yourself as a different person, a person different from you in fundamental ways. Imagining yourself as a different person can quickly free you to think in ways beyond your normal range of thought, to experience emotions beyond your normal range of emotions, as well as experience and learn from behaviors beyond your normal repertoire of behaviors. This one activity of regularly imagining yourself as someone else specifically different from you can become a deep well of creativity, from which you can draw at any time, for a multitude of purposes. It is a truly exciting, productive, encouraging and energizing activity which can be amazing fun, if you let yourself go. I mean that literally, but spelled with a slight difference: Let your self go. What is required is that you temporarily let go of your entire concept of your self, and as much as possible directly experience the world through the mind and heart and soul of someone else. Obviously, it is your imagination creating this experience, and so it is really still you, but the experience can be deep, and powerful, and an important lesson in just how potent your imagination can become, if you let it.

If you give serious thought to your own limitations as a person–not meaning this in a negative way or as an indication of inadequacy, but only as an acknowledgement that we are all limited in specific ways–it then makes clear sense to set about "designing" a person who fills in your gaps, who complements your other qualities, or who expands your range of emotion, understanding and behavior such that you are able to transcend your current limitations. You may choose to "design" several distinct people, according to what you want to accomplish, or in how you want to expand your self.

This act of imagination, this effort of imagination, can take many different forms. One of the fullest experiences of imagining yourself as a different person is to make the commitment to keep a journal for a certain period of time as though you actually are that person. Before you do that, you should construct a brief bio of the person you will be while making entries in the journal. Write in the journal whenever you want, as much or as little as you want. If you find yourself sinking deeply into the experience, that's good. Learn from all that happens during those times. You can also imagine yourself as a different person more casually, by simply taking some time to do so, in your own way. You also always have the option of either drifting freely in your imagination as a different person, or applying your imagination to a particular issue or problem in your life. This brings us to one of the most important reasons this effort of imagination is valuable.

We all behave differently with different people. In fact, for many of us, it's as though we have distinctly different personalities, depending on who we are with. The converse of that phenomenon is that other people behave differently with us than they do with people other than us. In part the reason for this has to do with our limitations. One implication of our limitations is that they have the effect of also limiting other people. At times, the best qualities in other people are unavailable to us, because our limitations do not allow those qualities to emerge. It's easy to think of examples of this. For instance, a pessimistic person will often have the effect of limiting the enthusiasm of others, or at least limiting the expression of that enthusiasm. A person who tends toward harsh criticism will limit the creativity of others, at least in the presence of that person. The tenderness a person is capable of will not be able to emerge in the presence of a person who, through their own limitations, instills fear in others. Such fear makes tenderness impossible.

Transcending our current limitations has the effect of allowing new possibilities to appear in our lives, partly in the form of positive qualities in other people. By regularly imagining yourself as a different person, with very different responses and attitudes, you can expand your awareness and perceptions as well as your range and flexibility of behavior. This has the effect of bringing out different qualities in other people, transforming your relationship with them, and presenting new opportunities.

Develop a deep relationship with art

"Stop thinking about art works as objects, and start thinking about them as triggers for experiences."

– Brian Eno

Perhaps you already have a deep relationship with art, or perhaps you don't. In either case, there may be aspects of art, ways of relating to art, or possibilities and opportunities within art of which you were not aware. Many people think of "art" mostly as something pleasant you may see hanging on a wall. Yet art is so much more than that:

PART TWO: DEEPER VALUES

- Art is a library of important ideas.
- Art is a gateway to new mental and emotional states.
- Art is a means of rising above yourself and your petty personal concerns.
- Art is a means of discovering and remaining aware of possibilities beyond the mundane.
- Art is personal transformation that's much less expensive than therapy, and much more fun.
- Art is a way of always reminding yourself and others that the way things are is not the way things must be.

All my life, I have relied on art not just to inspire me with beauty, but to expand my mind and my spirit, and always to help me become aware of the existence of possibilities which may not spontaneously occur to me. Whenever I become too preoccupied with my own situation and need greater perspective, I turn to art in its many forms—sometimes music, at other times visual arts, or dance, theater, film, literature, poetry. Each form of art has its own power, and its own possibilities. Art can also, in some cases, be a much better and much more reliable friend than any human being, offering solace, refuge, inspiration, stimulation and the ability to visit different worlds whenever you choose.

I encourage you to develop a deep relationship with not just one art form, but many, and according to the quote from Brian Eno at the head of this section: art as a trigger for experiences.

Acquire useful skills

A person with a large range of skills is much better off than a person with few skills, or no skills. It's a good idea to always be engaged in acquiring new skills, as well as improving and extending existing skills. Even more important is to be constantly thinking of and evaluating new skills to acquire.

There are many reasons to choose and develop and refine new skills. The reason most people think of first is employment, and yes, that's important. Other reasons include:

- Being able to help other people

- Being able to do something yourself, without paying someone else
- Being prepared for shifts in employment, or other areas of your life
- Keeping your mind and body active and vigorous
- Taking pride in your abilities
- Discovering new opportunities you couldn't possibly anticipate

Many skills that are truly important and valuable are not viewed as such by society. For instance, the ability to listen well, with both accuracy and empathy, is not generally valued by society, but is in fact a skill of great value which can create wonderful opportunities in your life, and the lives of others. Choose skills you believe are important, regardless of whether anyone else views them as important.

Invest in new capabilities
A capability is different from a skill. A skill is a particular way to do something. A capability means being able to do something at all. It's a larger category of ability. If you concentrate only on acquiring specific known skills, it may not occur to you to acquire entire new areas of capability.

For instance, it rarely occurs to people to work toward new emotional capabilities, yet emotional capabilities are a fundamental factor in success or failure in many areas of life. Becoming capable of greater courage and greater persistence can radically transform your life for the better. Becoming capable of deep, positive leadership can improve the lives of large groups of people. Many specific skills may be part of a larger capability, and it is certainly possible to gradually build a larger capability from a set of related skills.

Investing in new capabilities is directly related to the previous topic of expanding your identity. Expanding your capabilities will of course expand your identity, though a particular effect which often occurs in this process should be kept in mind; your identity may lag behind your capabilities. In other words, even once you have clearly acquired a new capability, you may find that your concept of yourself has not been updated accordingly. This can be confusing.

In my own life, after a certain point I worked very hard on acquiring the capability of being calm, or at least appearing to be calm, no matter what. Once I had mastered that capability, it was still a few years before I stopped apologizing for "getting so upset," when in fact I hadn't gotten upset. This was confusing not just to me, but to other people who had no idea what I was talking about. Eventually my identity caught up with the new reality, and I stopped feeling bad about something I wasn't actually doing any more.

I encourage you to think broadly–very broadly–about what new capabilities you would like to acquire. Please do not assume a capability is not possible for you, or is out of range for you. One of the problems with identity, and the reason I encouraged you to expand your identity, is that your current identity tends to limit what you consider possible, and even what you are aware of as possible. Someone who is currently very shy has trouble imagining themselves at ease with public speaking. For a person with a history of not finishing projects, it's a stretch to imagine themselves having already finished an entire large set of projects. Someone who tends to meekly agree, time after time, has great difficulty imagining themselves effectively and comfortably standing up for themselves and their actual opinions and feelings.

This is why it's so important to develop the specific capability of imagining yourself, deeply and completely and in detail, with additional capabilities. This type of active, productive imagination of yourself with new capabilities is a fundamental capability in itself, which helps to create other additional capabilities.

Build financial strength and flexibility

Most people get money, then spend it on stuff. They generally don't spend it on things that will help them in the long term, or will add valuable skills, or will help them take on important new capabilities. They just spend it on stuff–often stupid, useless, degrading stuff.

Eventually, this pattern catches up with them, and they find themselves locked into a set of structures in their life in which they have few options, and little room to maneuver. They're surrounded by stuff, often hemmed in by it, but the best possibilities they once had in their lives have been wiped away by all that stuff, including financial possibilities.

Financial strength and flexibility allow for much greater possibilities in your life. With financial strength and flexibility, you can immediately take advantage of possibilities which would be out of reach for many other people. You can rapidly create new conditions in your life to support a change you'd like to make, or a project you'd like to complete. You can say "yes" when you want to, and "no" when you need to, with confidence.

Building financial strength has many different aspects, but at the root of it is not discipline, as many people think. At the root of it is emotion. Why does one person strategically set money aside, while another compulsively spends? Emotion is driving both behaviors. Yet there is a direct connection between emotion and perception; change the perception, and the emotion changes. There is also a direct connection between perception and attention; what you pay attention to is what you perceive, which in turn affects your emotions. People who behave strategically in their finances are paying attention to very different things than people who just spend. You can fundamentally change your behavior by changing what you pay attention to.

I'll admit it; I have some challenges where desire is concerned. I once fell madly in love with a miniature chair of absolutely no practical value, but with a hefty price tag. I almost bought it, which would have been quite insane. Then I stopped for a moment, and chose to shift my attention. I wanted the chair. I was crazy for it. I also wanted my self-respect. I couldn't have both. I chose to pay more attention to my self-respect than to the chair, and so I now do not own a bizarre miniature chair, but I do still have my self-respect, at least where miniature chairs are concerned.

This is a minor example, but the principle is universal; change what you pay attention to and you will change what you perceive, and therefore what you feel. The change in what you feel then naturally changes your behavior.

Cultivate the virtue of frugality

When exactly was frugality moved from the "fundamental virtue" column to the "you must be a loser" column? Why was it moved from one column to the other, and by whom?

True frugality is a timeless virtue. This is because frugality means wise use of resources. To misuse resources or to use resources unwisely should never be seen as a virtue, yet during the twentieth century this is precisely what happened. With the invention of consumerism due to oversupply, the ubiquity of advertising, as well as the ubiquity of social pressure to conform, frugality was gradually assigned a negative value–as though not immediately spending all your money on the things you saw advertised was somehow a betrayal of your society.

PART TWO: DEEPER VALUES

Frugality is helpful in many ways, both material and spiritual. First, frugality is the basis for living within your means, so that you don't become captive to creditors. The positive way of putting this is that through frugality you can gain strong financial advantages. Second, frugality is an excellent way to practice discipline. The discipline of frugality strengthens your relationship with self-discipline and self-restraint in general, creating further advantages. Third, practicing frugality means constantly evaluating what is truly important in life, which has the effect of clarifying your values, and clearing your mind for the most important aspects of your life.

Frugality is a kind of curse word in modern society, but this particular "f-word" can give you much more than momentary pleasure. That's not what you'll hear from your society, however. If you begin to practice frugality, you may be perceived by others in ways that are not complimentary. Sarcastic references to "the last of the big spenders," being a "tightwad" or even "anal" should come as no surprise, given the relentless worship of senseless spending in our society. It is therefore advisable to be quietly frugal. Make your own decisions, share them judiciously, and beware of situations in which there will be intense pressure to spend money needlessly.

I once traveled to Reno with someone who, when we arrived, berated me when he discovered I had deliberately only brought $24, and didn't intend to spend a single penny on gambling. Noticing who mocks you for being sensible is an effective way to quickly discover who is worthy of your trust.

Cultivate the virtue of modesty

Observing our society in its current form, with its relentless and ubiquitous self-promotion by celebrities, politicians, sports figures, pundits and wealthy grotesque blabbermouths, one would never guess that modesty was ever considered a virtue. By modesty I mean not only the opposite of ostentation, which operates on an external level, but also the deeper, more significant form of modesty, which is an internal experience of humility. True modesty means a constant awareness that others are not as fortunate as you are, and that even your accomplishments are in a sense not entirely your own, because even if you worked hard and made sacrifices to achieve those accomplishments, your ability to do so was ultimately a result of the luck of the draw: your background, your genes, your good luck along the way. True modesty also means a fundamental understanding that we are all in this together, and that rubbing someone else's face in your privileges and good fortune is bad for our life together on this little planet.

That said, modesty also has distinct advantages. I'm not suggesting that you cultivate a false modesty in order to gain the advantages of apparent modesty, but as a matter of honesty if must be acknowledged that true modesty brings benefits. One clear benefit of genuine modesty is that because you won't be tempted toward ostentation, you won't be subject to the additional temptations the need for ostentation brings. The need for ostentation can be not only expensive, but can seriously warp your judgment, and get you into some bad, bad trouble. I grew up in a town chock-full of people mortgaged to the hilt on their McMansions in an effort to prove themselves to all the other McMansion mortgagees. Every once in a while one of them would commit suicide in some horrific way, after which it was revealed just how deeply they were in debt, due to their need for ostentation. Suicide is rather a big price to pay just to show off to people you probably don't even actually respect.

Another clear benefit of modesty is that you don't have to be a jerk, and thus don't have to waste time or lose resources on the blowback from being a jerk. That kind of blowback can deprive you of some of the best possibilities in life–good relationships, as the most obvious example. Modesty provides a clearer, more tranquil, more productive mind, which helps you to make better decisions. Modesty also promotes the ability to appreciate everything more deeply, and recognize valuable opportunities, because you aren't distracted by the wailing of your own ego.

Develop your relationships

Obviously, there is no direct contradiction between material possessions and relationships, and we all already have relationships of various kinds. In some cases possessions specifically allow for, make easier or enhance certain types of relationships. Yet most of us have either observed or been part of situations in which possessions interfered with relationships, or in which what we thought was one kind of relationship was eventually revealed to be based on possessions, and wasn't much of a relationship at all. It's easy to think of certain wealthy couples or celebrity couples in which the relationship was clearly more about the material trappings than about genuine relationship–all about the mansion and the cars and the gowns and the grossly expensive jewelry presented as tokens of a deep love that in fact is just the self-love and love of status the possessions represent. Many couples who longer have much of a relationship stay together only in order to preserve their material conditions; they preserve material status at the cost of personal stasis. There are people who form associations, sometimes of great intensity, based on a particular activity which in turn is based on possessions. I can easily think of many people who play video games obsessively with others, or play sports, who have no genuine relationship with each other, despite having spent many hours together in intense activity.

Which of your relationships are entirely free of reliance on possessions, or status? Who sticks by you, and appreciates you, even if you're down and out? If those questions made you wince, please think about exactly why. The details of the answers may be even more unpleasant than the original questions, but we're after the truth here, and the truth has its own profound value, and power to illuminate.

As a productive thought experiment, ask yourself who of the people you know would respond positively to the idea of spending time with you, without tying your meetings to consumption of any kind: just the two of you, together, for no reason other than to be in relationship to each other. Notice how many people are uneasy unless a meeting is based on some kind of consumption: eating in a restaurant; buying fancy wine or food; shopping of some kind; talking about products; electronic devices of various types; commercial events such as sports, concerts, movies. For many people, material possessions are a refuge from the unpredictability of human beings, and this is understandable; your computer almost always boots up in exactly the same way, but when you engage with a human being, you are usually rolling the dice as to their mood, level of distraction, current attitude, and emotional availability.

I don't mean to suggest an exercise in frustration and disappointment, but I would suggest that it is important to recognize which of your "relationships" are flimsy illusions, and which are true relationships. When I say "develop your relationships," part of what that means is discovering which of your connections with other people are genuine, and relatively free of dependence on material possessions, or even material conditions. You may quickly realize, if you haven't already, that your true relationships are few. Work toward complete clarity about who in your life is interested in and capable of genuine relationship with you, and then work to deepen and strengthen your relationship with them.

Give gifts of love, attention and understanding

In so many instances, there is nothing more precious or important than love, attention and understanding. This is partly because genuine love, attention and understanding are so rare. The level of self-involvement in our society has reached a level which is truly ridiculous, not to mention damaging, not to mention horribly tedious. Self-involvement in one person tends to produce self-involvement in other people, because the self-involved become unsatisfying as companions. Because the self-involved are bad listeners, and are bad at paying attention to others, those others can become frustrated and tempted toward self-involvement as their emotional needs are not met by the self-involved people around them. Along with this level of self-involvement has come the materialism which often produces personal alienation, emotional shallowness, emotional emptiness. The combination of these factors conspires to make love, attention and understanding more rare than they should be.

So make the choice, the conscious choice, to give gifts of love, attention and understanding. It may not be easy, for any number of reasons. You may get nothing in return–and in fact that is what you should expect–but you may also be surprised by where such a conscious choice can lead. There have been times in my life, in certain relationships, when I've done too much of the talking, and not enough of the listening. My choice to shift my attention fully to the other person and truly listen, and make a genuine effort toward deeper understanding of the other person, transformed the relationship all for the better. Efforts in this area can be daring and obvious, or subtle and barely detectable, but the crucial aspect is to consciously shift your attention as well as intention toward the other person.

Yes, even on holidays

Most of us would agree by this point that the period from Thanksgiving to January has become an official and socially enforced period of materialist insanity and materialist excess. How did we reach a condition in which it is socially required to buy a vast number of presents for other people, and that to not do so is seen as not only neglectful or unloving, but as a betrayal of our very economic system? Yes it's crazy, and yes, you can choose not to be part of it.

For years now, I have boycotted the materialist aspects of "the holiday season." I choose to not buy anything at all for anyone at all during that time, which has the effect of making any gift that I do send during the year a wonderful surprise, instead of a social obligation.

PART TWO: DEEPER VALUES

But consider this. What if instead of sending a material present at all, you did something else? What if you sent an invitation to an interesting experience you could share with another person? What if you sent a card saying "Let's spend more time together next year," or explained exactly what you like or admire about them? What if you sent a pledge to do something for them that you know would be helpful? What if, with someone you perhaps haven't treated as well as you should have, you promised to treat them better? Who in the world would be expecting a "present" as meaningful as a deeply felt apology? Any of those things would be far more interesting, and far more meaningful, than most of the presents people send each other during the holidays, many of which are actually unwelcome, or inappropriate, or awkward, or unnecessary, and many of which end up either neglected or abandoned.

Be creative. Be daring. Go deeper. Choose the truly interesting, the truly meaningful.

Yes, even on birthdays
Same deal on birthdays. Not every present has to be something you bought from a retail outlet. There are spiritual gifts, emotional gifts, gifts of intention, gifts of care and love and attention and understanding. Birthdays are particularly meaningful, because the day is intended to honor the particular person.

Recently it was a friend's birthday. What I did was very simple. I had asked months ago, with apparent casualness, when his birthday was. Then I put it on my computer calendar, and on his birthday I called him. That was all. We just talked for a few minutes on the phone, and he was surprised I even knew when his birthday was, and surprised and very happy to get the call. He recognized that I had deliberately asked for his birth date earlier, and recognized that I had made the effort to plan, and wait, and then make that simple call. It was also a recognition of his character, because he is not a person who would be impressed by any material gift.

So try it out. Give presents of a different kind, that aren't available on Amazon. I think you won't be the only person who will be happy you did.

Productive activities requiring little or no resources
Many of the most productive activities, activities that can lead to new opportunities in your life and can increase your capabilities in a way

that leads to even greater opportunities, require little or no physical resources. Most people behave as though the opposite is true: that everything important in life depends on material possessions. Their society has convinced them that they need to buy something in order to advance in any way, even though that's obviously false. Every advertisement you have ever seen, and by the time you've reached the age of eighteen you've seen tens of thousands of them, has in some way tried to convince you or make you feel that you are inadequate without the product they are trying to sell you, and that you can't make any progress on your own without such products.

The truth is that you can make much more progress on your own, much deeper and more significant progress on your own, using only your own mind and spirit, and your own effort. If you approach the activities listed below with the right attitude, they also become a matter not at all of effort, but of pleasure. The issue of pleasure entirely aside, each activity described below provides advantages in personal capability which can lead to wonderful opportunities.

Always think of something better to do

Most people, most of the time, operate on automatic. Their habits control them. They do the same sorts of things, over and over, and rarely if ever stop to think of something better to do, even though there is always a broad range of choices that would be much better than what they do out of habit. For example, far better than the habit of just plopping down in front of the television or doodling on the web or "chatting" with your friends is to cultivate the habit of insisting on thinking of something better to do–no matter what you're doing.

That's right, whatever you're doing, stop and think of something better to do. It may feel strange. You may feel at a loss, and you will almost certainly feel the strong pull of your habits. You may even awake to find yourself doing something you do habitually, having entered a trance induced by the habit, which made you forget that you were trying to think of something better to do. That's all normal, and part of the process. Take your time with this, considering many options. When you've gotten something much better to do clearly in mind, along with the reasons why it's better, think of something even better than that, along with the reasons. Complete at least three cycles of this. Even just three cycles will be quite difficult. If you can go further than that, by all means do so.

If you've done the exercise honestly and deeply, your head will be spinning, and you'll be truly embarrassed by just how much attention you have paid in your life to petty, idiotic junk. You may also be baffled, wondering why you never before thought of what you just thought of.

This is a hard exercise. You have to let go of your ego. You have to let go of some of your mental patterns. You have to let go of your attachments to your beloved junk. But the results, if you can do this exercise once a day or more, are fundamentally transformative to an amazing degree.

Seek out and ask yourself excellent, important questions

Excellent questions have their own power, their own ability to transform the way you think and feel, and the way you experience the world. A truly excellent question can change you deeply for the better, even when you have no idea how to answer the question. Many of the best questions do not have answers; the question itself is illuminating, and the more you ponder the question, the more illumination the question provides.

Most people encounter excellent questions at random, infrequently, and through no effort of their own. Consider this for a moment. Excellent, deep, productive questions always exist and have always existed, and are always available literally for the asking, yet most people make no effort to seek them out. Excellent questions are a free resource, not subject to copyright, and "making a copy" of an excellent question actually means being able to pass this free and valuable resource on to others.

Seek out and ask yourself excellent questions. Actively try to find truly wonderful, deep questions, and try to locate rich, reliable sources of such questions. Then engage with a question. Engaging with a question is different than trying to "answer a question." It's more a matter of exploring the question, aspects of the question, implications of the question, additional questions generated by the question, seeing where a relationship with the question leads, and how it changes or adds to your understanding or appreciation. Learn to distinguish between shallow questions and deep questions, between productive questions and unproductive questions, between expansive questions and constrictive questions.

If you find a few truly excellent questions, share them with other people, but judiciously; not everyone can appreciate excellent questions, and many people are frightened of questions of many kinds, and of deep questions in particular. Choose carefully the people with whom you share questions, and if you do choose carefully, you'll find that the best questions have the effect of encouraging collaboration, and of deepening bonds of meaning and trust. An existing friendship can be enhanced and deepened when you add engagement with deep questions to that friendship.

Learn to appreciate everything more deeply

If pleasure is one measure of quality of life, you can immediately and deeply improve your quality of life by choosing to appreciate absolutely everything in your life with greater depth, and greater detail. By "appreciation" I do not mean the usual call to be thankful for what you have. That's a different matter, and to me those exhortations to be thankful often come across as defensive, and sometimes as an obnoxious, indirect way of declaring ownership, or bragging. "See how much I have! Witness how very thankful I am for everything I have–everything that maybe you don't have, you measly schmo."

That's not what I mean by appreciation. I mean admiration for everything around you, deep curiosity about all the details of objects both natural and manmade, people, relationships, ideas, exploration of new aspects of all these things, and admiration for those newly discovered aspects in turn. Learning to become very good at this type of appreciation can be helpful in so many ways. Everyone has times during which the problems and challenges in their life weigh on them, and wear them down. Sometimes people become so involved with their own problems that they get stuck in a loop of dwelling on the problems, or even in a loop of self-involvement.

Deep appreciation can bring you out of that state quickly and reliably. You just have to become good at it, and all that takes is practice. Fortunately, there is never the slightest lack of material for appreciation because you are–and this is undeniable–completely surrounded by the universe. Even situations that are utterly screwed up can be deeply appreciated, and indeed should be, partly because you'll never be able to entirely avoid them and so you might as well make good use of them somehow, and also because in some ways the most screwed up situations contain the richest material, and the deepest lessons.

But absolutely anything will do. For example, pick up any small object nearby. Look at it. Feel it. Look at it more closely. Turn it

PART TWO: DEEPER VALUES

around in your hands slowly so that you see it from all different angles. If there are different light sources near you, look at the object under different light sources, and observe how its appearance changes in different light. Do you know exactly where it came from? Do you know how it was formed, and when, and where? Do you know exactly what it is made of? In all likelihood, all of the atoms in the object you are holding are billions of years old. The object itself may have been formed yesterday, but all the atoms that constitute the object were formed billions of years ago either in the center of a star during its life as a star, or during the explosion of a star at the end of its life. The atoms each traveled millions and millions of miles through interstellar space for a very long time, until they gradually aggregated as a tiny contribution to the total mass of the Earth. Some of those atoms may have been contained in meteorites or comets that struck the Earth in its early history, and were absorbed into its surface. In all probability, the object you are now holding contains atoms that were separated from each other for many years by many millions of miles in interstellar space, are now very close to each other. In another few billion years they will probably be blown apart again as our own sun ends its life, disintegrating our planet in the process.

How does that small object look to you now?

No matter what you are looking at here on Earth, all of these principles of origin billions of years ago, transit across the universe, and eventual aggregation as part of our humble planet apply. Nearly everything you see here on Earth was once part of a star that exploded. Your body is built from the byproducts of exploding stars billions of years ago. You are billions of years old already. Every atom in your body will be used again many times, in many ways, in some part of the universe.

How do you feel now?

That was just a simple demonstration of how to change your perspective on the objects you encounter in your daily life. I chose the cosmic perspective, because it's so surprising, and so effective at opening the mind quickly. There are many other ways to appreciate everything around you, particularly people, relationships, and your own imagination. I leave it to you to regularly devise new ways of deepening and expanding your appreciation of whatever you choose to appreciate. There is always more, and it is always ready.

Have fun thinking

Many people, because of negative experiences at school or for other reasons, never learned to have fun thinking. Some people even have negative associations with thinking, actively avoid thinking, and will even tell others harshly "You think too much." This is truly unfortunate, because thinking can be not only one of the greatest pleasures in life, but can produce dramatically positive results, and has the potential to fundamentally transform entire complex clusters of behavior for the better from a single, invisible thought.

Many people also have the mistaken notion that thinking is inherently abstract. Contradicting this is the fact that every product you've ever used or seen began as a thought: every can opener, filing cabinet, cruise ship, moon launch vehicle, computer monitor, screwdriver, condom, cochlear implant, pillowcase, air bag safety system, and yes, even every book like the one you're reading began as thought. Thinking is not abstract, but can be converted into material reality–and thinking can be very, very fun, if you do it right.

There are all kinds of thinking. Each one is its own special skill, and its own special pleasure. As an exercise in thinking, see how many different types of thinking you can think of. I can name at least fifteen types of thinking, without even thinking. :-)

If you don't have a good relationship with thinking, you're at a terrible disadvantage in many ways. Thinking is actually learning, so if you don't think, you don't learn. If you don't learn, you fall behind in life. If your relationship with thinking is not already strongly positive, I urge you to work steadily on learning to enjoy thinking. Try different kinds, and try to enjoy them all. Try to become good at all different kinds as well. Don't fall into a rut with just one kind. Some people become so good at analytical thinking that they become unable to think any other way, and that becomes a problem. You've probably known a few of those people. Others become so adept at imaginative thinking that they develop no skill at practical thinking, and this becomes tiresome as well as notably unproductive quickly, as you no doubt know as well.

Try to expand the range and depth of your capabilities in thought. Thinking is a skill, and like any skill grows with practice, and shrinks with neglect. Most of all though, enjoy all different kinds of thinking, in all different ways, and don't go stale. The more skilled you are at different kinds of thinking, the more quickly and effectively you'll be able to not only solve problems, but create wonderful new additions to your life and relationships.

Study a worthy subject in depth

Few choices are of greater value or greater significance than to study a worthy subject in depth. Given how obvious this is, the fact that so few people make the choice to do so is both remarkable and unfortunate. Further puzzling is the fact that it is so easy to identify a large number of worthy subjects, and immediately understand both the merits and the advantages of studying any of those subjects in depth. Yet again, so few people make that choice. Rather than dwell on the reasons so many people fail to make the excellent choice to study a worthy subject in depth, I will present just some of the reasons you should choose to be an exception.

First, study of a worthy subject is inherently interesting. Any subject which is truly worthwhile will be deep and detailed, will be engaging on multiple levels, and therefore will be profoundly satisfying, as well as illuminating. Next, any worthy subject will transform you as a person, all for the better. During your study of the subject, you will encounter important ideas and have important realizations which will expand your mind, expand your awareness, and increase your capabilities as a person. Further, deep study of any worthy subject both makes you yourself a more interesting person, and provides for more interesting exchanges with other people, particularly other people who have also chosen a worthy subject to study. On an even more advanced and extended level, genuine deep study of a worthy subject can lead to opportunities later on you can't even imagine when you first begin to engage with the subject.

How should you choose a worthy subject? There are many, many truly worthy subjects, though you'd never guess this from observing the conversation of most people. If you've never consciously given this idea serious thought, just keep asking yourself the question, keep the question in mind for a few days, and soon you will find yourself noticing consciously what you consider a worthy subject, as well as what you do not. (You will also probably begin to notice how few people are doing this, but are instead acting out of mindless habit.) Then begin to keep a list of subjects you consider truly worthy, and look your list over once in a while. This should not be in any way a dreary task, and is absolutely not a matter of studying something not of interest to you. You should only choose subjects of strong interest to you personally, and you should feel excited about doing so. You may also feel a bit strange, as though you are embarking on an unusual journey, probably alone. That is not a mistaken perception. You probably will be mostly alone in this journey, unless you can find a study buddy, or an online group, or some other way to regularly share what you are doing, and learning, and thinking, and realizing. Most people who choose this journey understand that the pleasures of the journey are mostly in the subject itself, though in most cases opportunities to share your knowledge will eventually present themselves, often at the most unexpected times, and unexpected ways.

Once you've chosen a truly worthy subject, think of approaches to learning more, approaches that suit you personally. Everyone is different in how they prefer to learn and explore. Choose the ways that work best for you. It's all right to change subjects, if you discover another you want to study more. You can also of course choose multiple subjects if you have enough time, and enough motivation.

This may surprise you, but I'd now like to ask a favor of you. If you do choose to seriously study a subject or more than one subject, once you begin to do so and are confident you will continue, let other people know what you are doing. Share both the idea of choosing a worthy subject to study, and share your knowledge. People may respond with interesting or unexpected questions which will deepen your interest in the subject. You will also be spreading this important idea of consciously choosing something important to study. If more people did this, we would have a better society, would all learn a whole lot more, and would have more fun talking with each other.

Replace bad habits with much better habits
We all have bad habits. I've had my share, and still do, though I have successfully eliminated many bad habits, and worked hard to identify and adopt good habits. Bad habits take many different forms, but some are much more serious than others. There are habits which are just minor behavioral patterns, like forgetting to wipe your feet or get the mail, but there are others which are much deeper and more significant, such as a bad emotional habit of taking things too personally, or indulging a bad temper, or not admitting fault, or never taking on challenges, or lying to yourself, not to mention lying to others.

Bad habits can drag you down, destroy opportunities, take over your life, and in the worst cases become so much a part of your identity that you actually begin defending and believing in things you never should have started doing in the first place. It's absolutely crucial to become truly skilled, truly competent and confident in not just getting rid of bad habits, but in cultivating excellent habits. This brings us to the subject of the relationship between good habits and bad habits, a relationship most people do not understand.

Too many people make the mistake of trying to directly eliminate bad habits. Trying to directly eliminate a bad habit only causes you to focus even more strongly on the bad habit; you end up paying attention to the bad habit, thus reinforcing it, instead of designing a new and much better habit to replace it. It's far more effective to think of an excellent habit you'd like to cultivate and master, which also happens to have the effect of eliminating a bad habit by replacing it with something much better. For instance, if you have a bad habit of mindlessly turning on the television and then wasting hours in front of it, trying just to "not watch television" is an idea that only reminds you of all the television you're not watching, with the result that the TV set is probably going to be getting turned back on. Instead, make sure you have much better things to do than watching TV, and understand exactly the reasons to be doing those things. Your mind will then be on those better things, not on all the television you're not watching.

Most habits take time to become fully established. The usual estimate for habits of moderate importance is three to six weeks, with constant application. I actually keep a spreadsheet of habits I am trying to establish, always expressed in positive form. When a new positive habit begins to take hold, I move it down to the bottom of the list, and put it in light grey. If I slip in establishing the habit, I put it back toward the top of the list, in black. When the habit is fully established and I'm confident it will remain part of my life, I finally erase it from the list. There are many helpful tips and tricks for establishing good habits, such as visualization, linking a new good habit to an already existing good habit, physical linking or "chaining" of behaviors through muscle memory or the senses, and matters of timing and systematic reinforcement. I encourage you to learn more about these subjects on your own. The previous section was on studying a worthy subject in depth. The subject of how to effectively and quickly adopt positive habits is certainly such a subject, worthy of study.

Seek out relationships specifically with people who give you new ideas and help you become a better, more capable person
Relationships are powerful. Who you choose to relate to and how you choose to relate to them have deep influences on you, and in many ways. Relationships can expand your view of what is possible in life, or contract and damage your view of what is possible in life. Relationships can make you a better person, or a worse person. Relationships can create new, expansive possibilities for you, or become a confining prison. Relationships can increase your capabilities, or cripple you.

Most people don't give this matter much conscious thought. By a combination of happenstance, convenience, attraction, and the pursuit of comfort, they end up with a set of people in their life they have not truly chosen. The people in their life have various qualities and various effects, and sometimes choices are made along the way to have less or more to do with one person or another, or to discontinue a connection with someone, but only rarely does anyone make a conscious choice, on a consciously examined basis, about exactly what qualities of mind and spirit they will seek in their relationships in general.

But ask yourself, "What will be the effect, in the long term, of not choosing what sort of person you include closely in your life?" The more important, positive form of that question is not "What qualities do I want in the people in my life?" but "What qualities in the people I choose to relate to would be good for me, and good for my life?" I make this distinction because if you base your decisions only on what you want, and no higher evaluation, certain mistakes will always occur. If you seek out only people who "make me feel good," you may be choosing a very long and comfortable road that leads absolutely nowhere–just a lazy, pointless dead end. If you seek out people you can always feel superior toward, you just signed a contract to not learn anything. If you seek out people who never question you about anything, who never challenge you, you might as well have a sign on your forehead that says "I refuse to grow."

Many people spend time with the same people, again and again, often in exactly the same ways, again and again. That might be comforting in its familiarity and repetition, but it's also a formula for stagnation and eventual decay. It can be challenging and even disturbing to examine your relationships and ask, regarding certain people, "What exactly is the effect of this person on me? Are they good for me? Are they holding me back?" The combination of the comfort of established relationships, feelings of loyalty, and fears of loss can conspire to prevent you from actively seeking out and establishing new connections with people who bring new ideas, attitudes and areas of interest into your life.

But you should do it anyway. Seek out people who expand your awareness, who bring rich perspectives, who present new and more noble possibilities for you and for your life.

Deliberately seek out exchange of valuable information
If you've ever stepped back and listened to most conversations, including perhaps your own, you've noticed how little information of value is in them, in general. Most conversations are not deep, or expansive, or productive, or illuminating. Nothing of deep value is learned from most conversations.

It doesn't have to be like this. You can choose to seek out valuable information in nearly every conversation, but you have to not only make that choice, but put in the effort of following through, and be brave about it. This doesn't mean being serious or intense in a way that puts other people off. It just means deciding that rather than do the usual thing of blabbing away without knowing why, that you shift your attention toward gaining genuinely useful knowledge and even insight from other people.

This is also not a matter of boycotting small talk, because small talk is often a way of putting people at ease, so that you can then proceed toward conversation of value. Every person has areas of knowledge, experience and insight which may be valuable to you, though with some people it's less obvious than with others. You have to do the work of opening your mind to types of value with which you may not be familiar, as well as the work of discovering those areas within other people.

This might sound like a lot of effort, but the payoff is huge in terms of knowledge, insight and even wisdom, and it sure beats having the same idiotic rounds of small talk that go nowhere, over and over again.

Thank anyone who deserves thanks
If you've ever had the experience of being thanked by someone unexpectedly, you know how good it can make you feel right away. You can make someone else feel that good in just a few seconds, and with just a few words. Do it. You may make a new friend, or form a new alliance. It's especially important to thank someone if you observe that they have made a big effort, but no one else has bothered to thank them. You know what that feels like, and you know how bad it feels.

So just step in and be the person who says "Thank you!" when no one else does. Then be on the lookout for the next person who could use some thanks, but isn't getting any, and then give them some. It's a great way to go through life, and you can make some wonderful connections along the way, as well as cheer people up, and bring just a little bit more justice into the world.

Give what you don't need to others individually, in the moment
As I mentioned in the introduction to the book, several years ago I made fundamental changes in my relationship with my possessions,

and my attitude toward possessions in general. One major change was in how I viewed possessions versus relationships, and possessions versus creative behavior. I noticed that certain people, even though their possessions exceeded the capacity even of their very large house, would make a big stink about even lending someone a minor possession. Most of us have had negative experiences with lending something that is never returned, or returned far too late, or returned with horrible awkwardness, or returned broken or damaged, accompanied by a lame excuse or worse, no explanation at all. It occurred to me how much better it would be to never lend anything, only give. That way you're never expecting anything back, and the eventual condition of the object is the responsibility of the new owner, and has nothing to do with you. I also saw creative opportunities in this new approach as well.

For instance, because so many people are tight-fisted about their possessions, few people are ever expecting you to just give them something. To do so, and particularly to do so casually, invites wonder and amazement, although it shouldn't, given the excess of possessions for so many people.

I chose to adopt the attitude that if something I owned would mean more to someone else, even just in the experience of unexpectedly receiving it, then it would be much better for them to get it than for me to keep it. I began to notice when someone took an interest in something I owned. Sometimes it was easy to notice. "Hey, where did you get that?" is a pretty reliable clue. Then all you do is hand them the object and say "It's yours." They will be momentarily confused. They will resist. They may offer to pay you. They may say "I can't." Just explain to them that it would be more interesting for both of you for them to take it and keep it, and that the experience will be an interesting bond in your relationship. It's actually a way of saying "I want an interesting connection with you," which is a beautiful compliment.

I began to take this even further, and I'm very glad I did. For instance, at one point I owned three different shoulder packs, of different designs. One had a single wide band that rested on one shoulder, and wrapped loosely around the body, allowing you to wear it on your back, but at any time swing it around to the front and open it up, without ever taking it off. It was a cool little pack. One day someone stopped me in the street, and asked me where I had gotten the pack. He told me that he had once had one, but it had been stolen, and he hadn't been able to find a replacement. He was very frustrated about the theft, and about not being able to find a replacement.

We finished talking, and he walked away, but he hadn't gotten fifty paces before I realized what I had to do. I walked back over to him, handed him the pack, and told him to keep it. He was stunned. It was a brand new pack, just like the one that had been stolen from him. He needed it much more than I did, so he was the one who got it. The value that was created in that simple exchange was far greater than the value of the pack; he got relief from the bitter memory of the theft of his pack, the frustration of not being able to find one like it, and we both got a wonderful, quirky, inspiring memory. Every time I think of that stranger using the pack, I can't help breaking into a big smile. He probably has similar feelings. That was a very good deal, for both of us.

Be creative. Give stuff away, as opportunities come up. Try to create new value by handing your stuff over to people you know, or even people you don't. You'll probably be creating value much greater than the value of the stuff itself.

Don't watch television–at all

This is the only item in the list that is a "don't" not a "do." Yet in not doing this, in not watching television, you are in fact doing many things of major importance:

- Making room in your mind for more important matters.
- Clearing out some of the junk that clogs your mind.
- Making more time for things in your life that matter much more.
- Exercising your freedom of choice.
- Developing a critical perspective on your own society.
- Gaining more self-respect.
- Withdrawing your support from a corrupt, unhealthy system.
- If you cancel your cable service, you're saving money.
- You may even end up thinner, and with a smaller butt.

There are many good reasons to never watch television. If you have the habit of watching television, don't kid yourself that you're doing anything worthwhile, because you're not. Don't defend your favorite shows, because they're really not that great. Don't make excuses, such as saying "But it's my way of relaxing," because there are far better ways to relax than by filling your mind with inherently undignified junk. Choose something much better to do, and make that a habit instead. If you're not convinced, please read on.

One day, you hear about a grocery store where lots of people shop. In fact, many people seem to spend lots of time there, sometimes as much as four or five hours per day. You hear, to your amazement, that some people spend as much as seven hours per day in this grocery store. You find that quite strange, but you figure you'll give it a try. Maybe the store is just so wonderful that people want to spend seven hours per day there. Who knows?

You head over to the grocery store, but then you find something even more strange; the store wants to charge you more than $50 per month just for the privilege of shopping there. Then you discover something still more bizarre; the actual point of this grocery store is to hypnotize you into wasting your money buying all kinds of stuff you don't actually need. In fact, the entire purpose of the store is precisely to get you to buy stuff you don't need that's actually bad for you. But you decide, what the hell, it seems to be so popular, I'll give it a go. Can all these people shopping in the store be wrong?

You enter the grocery store, and the first thing you notice is the stench of all the rotting food. It hits your nostrils like a sharp knife. You're amazed that anyone would actually choose to eat any of this clearly unhealthy, in fact dangerous stuff. You endure the stench and the filth and obvious presence of dangerous bacteria for several minutes, and finally find a tiny 1% of what is being offered that is barely edible, but the store itself is so horrendous you can barely stand to be there, and you are concerned about your own health simply from the exposure.

That's television. It's not healthy. Get the hell out of there.

Conduct focused, valid and worthwhile research on the web

Most people use the web by now. However, most people use it badly. By this I mean they not only use the web without much skill, but they also use it mostly for shallow entertainment, trivia, escapism and worse. If used in this way, the web can be even worse than television. Yet the web remains the most valuable resource of information by far in all of human history. The web is always there, ready for you to use it in specific, focused, productive ways.

If you are not already highly skilled at doing research on the web, one of the first projects you should undertake is to learn techniques to use search engines with greater control and flexibility. To start, search on "techniques for using search engines." You will get a large number of results. Look through the first page or two of results and pick two or three results that appear to offer instruction in search techniques. Study these techniques, try them yourself, and then include them in your regular use of search engines. You may be amazed by how much more relevant the results of your searches become. If you learn only one new, simple technique per week for six weeks, you will soon become very adept at finding exactly what you want, with little guessing.

Next choose a truly worthy subject about which you'd like to know more. Apply your new search techniques, and create a folder for browser bookmarks with a name based on the subject you'll be studying. When you find web sites or documents you want to set aside for study, save them in the bookmarks folder. It's a good idea to get used to saving each bookmark with the best name possible, because the default name may not represent the content very well; you can almost always come up with a name which will work better for you when you are looking through your collection of bookmarks.

A technique that I have found very helpful is to cut and paste information from web sites and documents into a word processing file. I cut and paste freely, then sweep back and organize and condense all the information in that one file. The work of organizing the information is a natural way of learning the information in detail, and the highly organized document also makes later review very convenient and efficient.

Read books from the library

Your local library is one of the best deals on the planet, and remember that you've already paid for it through your local taxes, so not using it is by definition a waste of your money. Even the smallest library has books containing valuable information with which you can enhance your life, advance your career, and spend many productive hours in learning and enjoyment. Reading books of high quality is one of the most important habits you can ever develop in your life. Many libraries having cooperative sharing agreements with other local or regional libraries, so the books you see in the library itself are in many cases only a small portion of what is actually available to you. Ask the librarian whether your library is connected to other libraries, and if so how to search the entire set of holdings of all the cooperating libraries. You may be amazed by what you find. Learning how to search effectively using the library's computer system is a small investment in time, but with a big payoff.

Many libraries have an acquisition budget, which means you can request that they buy certain books. If you already use Amazon or other services to buy books, a handy technique is to research books on line through such services, then find out if the books are already available at the library, and if not, request that the library purchase the book.

A single caveat where use of the library is concerned: make sure you master the habit of returning books on time, or renewing on line or over the phone, so that you retain good standing with the library, and don't incur any late fees. If you're a slob about this, you can get badly burned financially.

Keep in mind that you need not check out books to make good use of the library. Many people do much of their reading in the library itself, or go just to explore the books and other holdings. Wandering through the stacks, subject by subject, taking down books that catch your eye and reading only the table of contents can be quite an education in itself. Because the books are filed systematically by subject and sub-area, you can gain a good understanding of the structure of entire large areas of knowledge just by wandering the stacks and noting the hierarchy of classifications within an area of knowledge. Using this method, you can also quickly gain an understanding of how important certain subjects are, by the number of books devoted to that subject.

One of my favorite activities is wandering into a library, then wandering into the stacks at random, observing the organization of knowledge, and admiring the books. I love looking at books in subjects about which I know little or nothing. This is always a humbling experience, one that invites me to open and expand my mind. I also find this an implicit form of prayer of thanks to all the people throughout the ages who made such enormous efforts to record, organize and make available the world's knowledge.

Decide on something truly productive to imagine
Imagination often gets a bad rap, in many ways. As children, many of us were criticized for "daydreaming" or having "too active a fantasy

life." Later we may be told that we are "impractical" or that we "ask stupid questions" or "think too much." Much of that criticism we experienced as discouragement of imagination, of productive fantasy.

Yet without imagination, most of what human beings have created would never have been developed, or even gotten started. Imagination is the starting point for much of what is best in life. It's important to remember that, especially if life becomes so hectic that time and energy for imagination is hard to find.

Many people tend to think of imagination as something that happens spontaneously, and at unexpected times. This certainly can be the case, and often is. Most of us have had the experience of a sudden realization occurring on its own at an odd time, even when we were thinking of something else; the realization or imagination breaks into our consciousness before we quite know what's happening, or why.

That's one kind of imagination, but only one, and such experiences can give us the mistaken idea that imagination must always be spontaneous. My view is that imagination should never be the slave of spontaneity. Imagination is a skill, one that can be developed, deepened and extended with practice, and even invoked at will.

My own imagination was always strong, but I also worked hard to develop it much further. I never accepted the idea that I was at the mercy of unpredictable, "spontaneous" miracles of imagination. Why would anyone choose to be so helpless? No, I insisted that my imagination be ready whenever I needed it, and that meant practice. I also learned to distinguish between freely wandering imagination and focused imagination. They are two distinct types of imagination, both valuable, but quite different from each other: different in nature, different in their purpose, and different in where and when they should be applied.

Freely wandering imagination begins with no specific goal, other than to experience a journey the nature of which cannot be anticipated. Focused imagination begins with a specific goal, and applies imagination toward ways of achieving that goal. Do not mistake one for the other. Freely wandering imagination is very useful for broad exploration and broad discovery, for the occasional unexpected insight, and for discoveries about your own mind and spirit. Focused imagination is more practical, and more specific, though in no way more limited than freely wandering imagination. I am in favor of developing both types, primarily because truly original accomplishment requires both types.

If a person is only capable of freely wandering imagination, they have a serious deficit, because they are unable to imagine the steps to transform what they imagine into practical reality. We've all known such people; they sometimes have truly wonderful ideas, but they are unable to act on their ideas in a practical way. However, a person who is only capable of focused imagination also has a deficit, because they are unable to develop original ideas in the first place. Obviously, having true gifts in either of these areas is rare, and having gifts in both areas even more rare. Yet the mistake many people make is to believe that imagination cannot be developed. It can be developed, and developed to an amazing extent, with practice.

Bringing together the idea that imagination should be at your service, and that you should become adept at both type of imagination, I invite you to set aside specific times to exercise your imagination. As you become better and better at using your imagination in different ways, you'll also become more skilled at knowing exactly how to apply it. There will be times when you know you should allow your imagination to range widely, even wildly, such that you are surprised or even shocked by what emerges from within your mind. This is the time to suspend all judgment, and just let the ideas arrive in whatever way and in whatever form they happen to take. There will be other times when you know that you must switch to practical imagination in order to map out and accomplish particular tasks. This type of imagination requires that you exercise sound, accurate judgment. After all, you're working to imagine with complete accuracy the steps you will have to take to get something done, using your time, energy and other resources, including money, as efficiently as possible.

Let your mind to drift, and watch what it does, and tends to do

When I mention to this to most people, they immediately say, "Oh, you mean meditate." No, I don't mean meditate. I mean watch your mind, watch it carefully, take note of both what it does and what it tends to do, as well as what it doesn't do and tends not to do. Then deliberately form judgments about what you discover, and develop projects to expand, adjust, train and exercise your mind.

Most people have not made much of a study, to any deep degree, of their own mind. They assume, for instance, that they are responding to "reality," when it would be much more accurate to say that they are responding only to the tiny sliver of reality represented by repeated perception only of the patterns they have previously learned to perceive, which patterns themselves may or may not match reality closely at all. Many people mistake their preoccupations for reality, though reflection for only a moment will make clear to you that a preoccupation is by definition a major distortion of reality through a combination of excessive emphasis and exclusion. Many people are entirely unaware of major biases embedded so deeply in their mind that the thought has never occurred to them that much of what they experience as direct perception is only the operation of their own biases.

There is much to know, much to study, and much to question about the workings of one's own mind. A dedication to observation of one's own mind–its habits, its tendencies, its strengths and weaknesses, its gaps, areas of rigidity and flexibility, its aversions, its compartments and leakage and tricks of hiding aspects of itself from itself, and from you, its many states and what they mean and why they happen–and encouragement of a questioning attitude toward one's own mind, can become a truly powerful generator of new ideas and new mental and emotional capabilities. Studying your own mind with both affection and a critical attitude can bring you very, very far.

If you haven't done much of this, I'd suggest you not only get started soon, but make a deep habit of it. Make it part of your daily life, and your experience moment to moment. If you do develop this skill strongly however, there is a second skill you'll also need, and that is to be able to stop doing this whenever you want to; be able always to give yourself completely to the details of every moment, as appropriate. Few people are more irritating or less productive than those trapped in their own mind. Develop the ability to move back and forth fluidly between watching your own mind, being completely self-conscious in a literal sense, and completely at one with the moment, not watching your own mind at all. How will you know which state you should be in? You learn, that's all. You keep learning, and you keep getting better at it, better at choosing when your focus should be inward or outward, or rapidly alternating, depending on the situation.

Exercise: What goes on?
Lie on your back in the middle of the room, spread eagle, relax for a few minutes, and try to think of nothing. You won't be able to, no matter you hard you try. So just allow anything at all to appear in your mid, take note of it, and take note of how you react. Simply observe,

without judgment of any kind, and take note. That is all. Repeat as appropriate.

Deepen your relationship with the natural world

Many people have a seriously underdeveloped appreciation of and relationship with the natural world. They are deprived of all the inspiration, deep admiration and joy that comes from an ongoing relationship with the natural world in all its forms. Instead, they are tied up in matters exclusively human, mostly narrow, often petty. They have no idea at all that they are missing nearly the entire Universe, and all its miracles.

There is an obvious relationship between senseless acquisition of possessions and exclusive orientation toward human social life. After all, our entire society is structured to encourage material acquisition, and discourage serious thought or reflection. Most of the people you know are unconscious promoters of thoughtless materialism, because they too are embedded within and under the influence of the social system. Because society is unfortunately inimical to the natural world, even though ultimately dependent on the natural world, one of the ways you can free yourself from the bonds of conformity within society is by forming a deep relationship with nature. This relationship can take an infinite number of different forms, any and all of which are valuable.

I was fortunate to grow up in an area with a great variety of natural environments. Woods were just out the back door, a river ran through town, my neighborhood was dotted with freshwater ponds, and there were three saltwater beaches within walking distance. I got to meet many, many fellow creatures of all kinds, from bluefish and striped bass and river flounder to frogs and turtles, owls and egrets, praying mantises, butterflies, beetles and beautiful bugs I never learned to name. I grew up studying the colors, feeling the textures and breathing in the smells of hundreds of different types of plants. I used to walk for hours through town, at all times of day and night, just taking it all in, with all of my senses. When I later discovered just how troublesome and disappointing human beings can be, all those deep experiences of the natural world became my refuge and salvation. It's terribly easy to find falsity in people, but hard to find falsity in nature. It's terribly easy to find pettiness in people, but hard to find it in nature. Occasionally, though rarely, you can find inspiration in people, but you can always find inspiration in nature, because nature is infinite. Nature means complete freedom from the prison complex of human social norms.

So I invite you to deepen your relationship with the natural world, in any way you choose. Who knows? You might even meet a friendly little fish, have an illuminating conversation, and agree to stay in touch for an ongoing exchange of views.

Work to fully understand your body
Your body is a complex instrument, with many capabilities, and many patterns of response. Your body is also remarkably changeable in many ways. Evolution provided the ability for your body to adjust to myriad demands: changes in food supply, level of activity, degree of strength required, degree of flexibility, tolerance of cold and heat, level of stamina.

PART TWO: DEEPER VALUES

Most people do not know their own body well at all. They only know the basics of how it responds and what it is capable of within the narrow range of their usual activities. They have no idea what else it can do, or how much it can change in response to new conditions, new demands, particularly if those new demands are applied over long periods of time.

Gaining a deeper and more detailed understanding of your own body is a valuable investment, in several ways. First, you will discover that your body is capable of much more, a great deal more, than you probably ever imagined. This is a source of great confidence. Second, your body is so changeable that you can deliberately mold and train your body in ways which can help you accomplish important goals, contribute to a positive outlook, and give you more confidence. Third, knowing exactly how your body responds to various conditions improves your judgment in setting goals and gauging how you will function in various situations. Fourth, once you have experience in changing your body to meet particular needs, you increase the depth of your understanding of what else is possible, and also enhance and deepen your imagination.

This subject is yet another that could easily fill an entire set of books, so I will end this section with only a few suggestions of areas to explore. For each area, if you choose to discover what your body is capable of, do so judiciously. This is not an exercise manual. Proceed carefully and with good judgment, at your own risk. The important lesson here is not to "get in shape" in a particular way, although that may be something you choose to do. The truly important lesson is to gain experience with what your body is capable of, particularly beyond the limits of your current habits, and the current conditions in your life. If you persist, you will probably be amazed by how much more your body can do, and how much it can change, and how much you can change it, given the right demands over time.

- Strength: How much can you change the strength of parts of your body?
- Stamina: How much can you increase your stamina in various ways?
- Flexibility: How stretched out can you get, if you work at it gradually but persistently?
- Amount of fat: How much can you change this? What's required?

- Body shape: How much can you mold your body, with the right plan and enough consistency and persistence?
- Coordination: How much skill in coordination can you achieve, and in what skills?

Improve your health

Your health is precious. Many people don't truly understand this until they have a serious health problem. Many people also accept a level of health that is much lower than optimal. They accept having lower energy and stamina than they could have, and accept feeling either bad or not very good, when they could be feeling great.

Your good health should not be taken for granted, particularly if you have bad habits which affect your health. In addition, what is required to maintain your health at a high level is different at different points in your life. Investing in knowledge about how to promote and maintain your health is one of the best choices you can make.

Invest in knowledge of nutrition

The good news about nutrition is that by following a few fundamental guidelines, you can radically improve your nutrition without spending vast amounts of time studying, or spending ongoing time planning for each meal, or doing anything as absurd as counting calories.

I encourage you to explore the subject of nutrition, and decide on a few guidelines you believe would help you maintain and enhance your health. I also encourage you to steer clear of anything too complex, or burdensome. Eating a healthy diet should be a physical pleasure, not a mental burden.

In my own life I follow only a few dietary guidelines, but these few guidelines have helped me maintain excellent health throughout my life, without having to spend a lot of time researching all the details of the vast variety of foods:

- Prefer a natural diet, which means prefer unprocessed food over processed food. The mainstays of my diet are things you could pick directly off a tree, or directly out of the ground.
- Eat lots of different things, the more variety the better. This applies both to your overall diet, and to individual meals. In any case, don't fall into a pattern of eating the same small number of

things again and again. Explore, sample, add constantly to your nutritional repertoire.

- If you can avoid the pesticides and additives, do so, even if it costs a bit more. Don't make a fetish of it, but do make an effort.
- If you've ever seen it advertised, don't eat it. Following this one guideline will radically improve your diet. In our society, unfortunately, the most heavily advertised products are usually the least healthy. Conversely, the healthiest foods get little or no advertising. Organic fruit, vegetables and dairy products will not be featured in ads during the next Super Bowl.

Invest in knowledge of exercise
Good nutrition without exercise is only halfway healthy. There are so many ways to get good exercise, and so many ways which are enjoyable and enhance your life. If exercise seems to you a dreary chore, you've been doing the wrong kind of exercise, or you have associations with exercise that aren't helping you.

It's a good idea to think very broadly as to ideas for exercise. Don't get stuck on thinking the gym is your only option. There are many, many options, most of them much more fun and requiring less time and hassle than going to the gym. Notice that the ways most people think of to exercise have their basis in someone selling something, such as a gym membership, or special exercise equipment.

When I say "invest in knowledge of exercise" I don't mean buy some exercise books, or sign up for aerobics or Tae Bo classes or hire a personal trainer, although any of those would surely provide good exercise. I mean invest some time and attention in learning more about options for exercise, but most of all learning about your own individual body and what exercise is most enjoyable and beneficial for you personally.

As in the previous section on diet, I strongly encourage you to give the matter some thought, and decide for yourself on a few guidelines for exercise that will be helpful to you individually. Human bodies are very diverse, so no single set of guidelines will suit everyone. Beware of exercise chauvinism, and exercise chauvinists. There are people whose egos are so attached to certain forms of exercise and certain "accomplishments" in exercise as they see it, that you may find the form of exercise you prefer denigrated or derided, even though it's actually perfect for you. Ignore the exercise chauvinists. Decide on your own forms of exercise, based on what works best for you, and explore further as suits you.

Many activities count as exercise which you will not find in books on exercise. Gardening is one. Playing frisbee is another. Just walking is excellent, gentle exercise. One of my favorite forms of exercise is picking up trash wherever I go. I walk quickly, carrying a plastic bag, usually a bag I just found discarded on the street, a bag which was just another piece of trash itself until I turned it into a bag to pick up trash. I make a game of chasing down all the litter in an area, and within about fifteen minutes of walking quickly and bending down to pick things up, I'm breathing hard, and in a light sweat. It's a very good workout, as well as a public service that may inspire other people if they happen to see you in action. I get lots of people thanking me, beeping an waving from cars, and even joining me in this modest public service. Try it some time.

Change your state by means of your body

The mind and the body are intimately linked, and neither is dominant. Your body influences your mind, and your mind influences your body. This simple observation has important implications, which many people fail to understand, and fail to use to their advantage. For instance, you can easily affect your mental state, your mood, your level of mental energy, by changing your posture, or your facial expression. Those two approaches, however make use of only the smaller muscles of the body, and not in a vigorous way. You can make much deeper and more powerful changes in your emotions and mental state through stances, positions and movements which make use of the larger muscles in a more vital way. Try this:

Lie down in a fetal position, one arm wrapped protectively around your legs, while sucking the thumb of the opposite hand. Do you feel strong, aggressive, and dominating? No, I didn't think so. Now stand up, take a wide stance, spread your arms out wide, lean forward, open your mouth wide as though preparing to bite someone, and scream loudly while waving your arms vigorously. Do you feel meek and gentle? Ok, you get my point; you can very quickly change your internal state by changing your external state. There are deep lessons in this, lessons our society has forgotten, but which you should remember.

Want to feel a certain way? Then move that way. It's nearly impossible to move using the large muscles of your body without producing a corresponding internal state. Recently it was discovered, for instance, that one of the most effective treatments for depression was simply to walk quickly, on a regular basis. That's a truly important example, because so many people suffer from depression, but there are infinite additional ways you can use the principle of outward movement to create inner state. Another quick example: If you're feeling tense, you're probably hunched over, one way or another. If so, stand up, assume a comfortable wide stance, slowly bring your arms up to a forty-five degree angle above your shoulders, slowly lean back, and wave your entire torso and arms gently, as though a gentle breeze is moving your body. Keep doing that for a little while, breathing slowly and deeply. Within less than thirty seconds, you will probably feel very different, less tense, and considerably better.

Invent productive, fun activities with other people, minus stuff

What if you could radically increase the quality of your life without spending a single penny more? Well, you can. In fact, that's the fundamental idea in this book. Still, it's up to you to devise the best ways to go about this, based on your own wishes, abilities and resources. Keep in mind, however that not only can you evaluate your own wishes and choose different wishes which serve you better, but you can also increase your own abilities, and improve and add to the resources available to you. The wishes, abilities and resources you already have are always open to improvement.

For the moment though, please just begin making mental notes about activities with other people which are both fun and productive, and which require little or no stuff. The most obvious area is in developing and deepening your relationships. You could work on having better conversations (a deep and complex topic in itself), or increasing the level of trust and confidence in your relationships, or adding creativity to your interactions, or adding interesting challenges. Another idea is to simply choose or favor activities which involve no particular material requirements. Many a meal is taken alone that could be taken in productive companionship. You're going to eat anyway, so why not make it more interesting, and add some new possibilities? Likewise, and I know this sounds simple, but any area you walk could be an area you walk with others.

One of the richest areas to explore is that of your own potential behavior. Each one of us, to a terrible extent, is merely a collection of habits in our interactions with others. Mostly without realizing it, we restrict and confine the possibilities between us and other people, simply through the limitations inherent in our habits of interaction.

Every new behavior has the potential to create new opportunities for relationship and exploration with others. Try out new behaviors, observe what happens, and then try out additional new behaviors based on what you discover. Of course there will be some awkward moments, and a few disasters, but the exploration itself is tremendously worthwhile because of what you will learn, and because exercising your imagination in this fundamental area of imagining yourself behaving differently is the most important gateway to personal freedom and the ongoing creation of new possibilities in your life.

Become a certified stuffologist

Ok, there's no such thing as a certified stuffologist, though perhaps some day there will be. But that doesn't mean you can't make use of the concept right now, share it with others, and spread the illumination it brings.

What would it mean to be a certified stuffologist? What would the science of stuffology entail, exactly? What would be included in the curriculum of a certification program in Advanced Stuffology?

I strongly recommend that you develop such a program, make the program truly rigorous, put yourself through it, certify yourself, and then begin introducing yourself as a Certified Stuffologist. Naturally, you will get a few inquiries as to what a Certified Stuffologist is and does. You will be in a very strong position to respond to such inquiries, because you will be one of the few world experts in this exciting new area.

:-)

PART TWO: DEEPER VALUES

Thank you

Thank you so much for reading this book. I hope you found it interesting, and I hope it has been helpful to you. By now you understand my attitudes toward possessions, so the request which follows will not surprise you. If you have a hard copy of this book, and you're done with it, please give the book away to someone. If you like the ideas in the book, please pass the ideas on to others as well. Ideas, like love, are one of the few things you can give away and still have.

If you would like to get in touch with me, please write or call:

firinn@livingmuchmore.com
(925) 478-5216 (United States)

I would also very much appreciate your reviewing the book on Amazon, or anywhere else it appears. I'm not asking for positive reviews, just honest reactions. That's what is best for everyone.
Thank you again, and best of luck, discovery, illumination and pleasure on your journey!

Web site for Living Much More

The web site accompanying this book contains additional materials:

- worksheets optimized for printing
- the exercises in the book, optimized for printing
- other supplemental materials
- updates
- contact information
- pictures from the appendix "A few favorite possessions"

http://livingmuchmore.com

Appendix: A few favorite possessions

It is true that by choice I own much less than most people, but this is partly because I have chosen my possessions with such care. Below are my favorite possessions, nearly all of which are small, and required minimal resources from the natural world. If I lost all of these possessions at any moment, I wouldn't care a bit, but I appreciate them every day.

- An emu egg, broken open. It is very large, deep shades of green, with a rough surface. I bought it at the farmers' market in town, and used it to make an enormous omelette one morning. Though its contents were surprisingly bland, the egg shell itself is dramatic, and beautiful.
- A collapsible book case from Brazil, finely crafted and sturdy, but with hinges inside, allowing it to fold completely flat for transport, like a wooden piece of origami. You would never guess this from its appearance.
- A German edition of Scriabin Preludes, Op. 11. The cover is the deep blue of all Henle editions, and the composer's name is in the German spelling, "Skrjabin."
- A slice of sedimentary rock which I use as a coaster by my bed. It contains many shades of yellow, orange and brown, in soothing, flowing shapes.
- Two sodalite bookends. Sodalite is a deep blue stone, streaked with white. The book ends are polished on only two sides, so you can appreciate both the rough and polished forms of the stone. I have the left bookend with the rough side facing out, the right bookend with the polished side facing out.
- Six short pieces of copper wire which I found by the dumpster and stripped with a knife, almost losing the end of a finger in the process. I tied the bare copper pieces together at one end with the shortest piece of copper, then bent the other pieces at the other end to make a copper flower.
- A piece of Orthoceras, a genus of extinct nautiloid cephalopod. It is a stark black, grey and white. Hundreds of millions of years ago that little bastard was alive, and prowling around in the ancient ocean.

- A solid aluminum tape dispenser from Denmark, which I rarely use but has an exquisite shape. It's more a beautiful sculpture than a tape dispenser.
- A small solar powered clock which has recharged itself from ambient light with no maintenance for more than eight years.
- A feather from a red-tailed hawk. I found the feather on the sidewalk.
- Three kinds of pine cone I found in various places nearby.
- A wrapped bunch of lavender, given to me by a kindly man who runs a small shop in Mali Losinj, Croatia. Four years later, it still has a lovely, faded scent.
- Two solar ovens which I use to cook many of meals, nine months of the year.
- A small bunch of dried statice I bought years ago, which has lost all its color but contains beautiful shapes. I seek statice, not status.
- A small Meyer lemon tree, the lemons from which I slice up and put in yogurt, rind and all. Absolutely delicious. Thanks, little tree.
- A beautiful small bird house, which I hung under the eaves near the head of my bed. One very cold January a juvenile Nuttal's Woodpecker began roosting in the bird house each night, only a few feet from where I slept. Every afternoon about five o'clock he would perch in a nearby tree and call for a couple of minutes, then head into the bird house for the night. For a full month, every night, I had a young avian bedtime companion, who was struggling to survive to adulthood through the cold winter. Some nights I would wake up and shift in bed, and hear the young bird shift as well inside the bird house. The weather finally warmed, and one night my friend did not return. But I still see and hear him around the neighborhood. He's bigger now, and certainly could no longer fit in the opening to the bird house. Knowing he made it to adulthood because of that bird house warms my heart.

Pictures of these possessions can be found on the web site:

http://livingmuchmore.com

www.ingramcontent.com/pod-product-compliance
Lightning Source LLC
Chambersburg PA
CBHW071511040426
42444CB00008B/1592